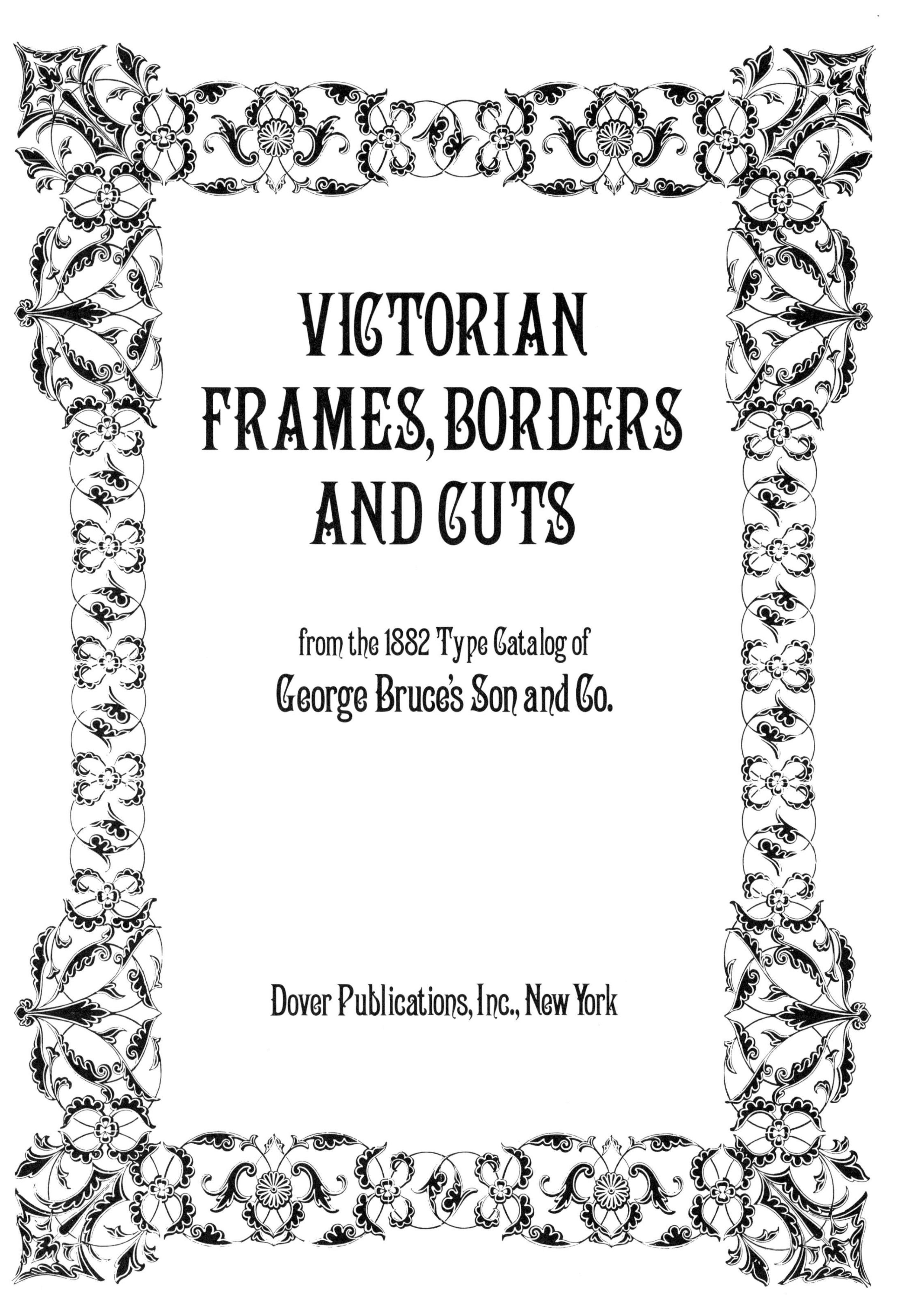

VICTORIAN FRAMES, BORDERS AND CUTS

from the 1882 Type Catalog of

George Bruce's Son and Co.

Dover Publications, Inc., New York

Published in Canada by General Publishing Company, Ltd., 30 Lesmill Road, Don Mills, Toronto, Ontario.

Published in the United Kingdom by Constable and Company, Ltd.

***Victorian Frames, Borders and Cuts,* first published by Dover Publications, Inc., in 1976, is a new selection of material from *Specimens of Printing Types* published by George Bruce's Son and Company, New York, in 1882.**

DOVER *Pictorial Archive* SERIES

International Standard Book Number: 0-486-23320-0
Library of Congress Catalog Card Number: 75-46418

Manufactured in the United States of America
Dover Publications, Inc.
31 East 2nd Street
Mineola, N.Y. 11501

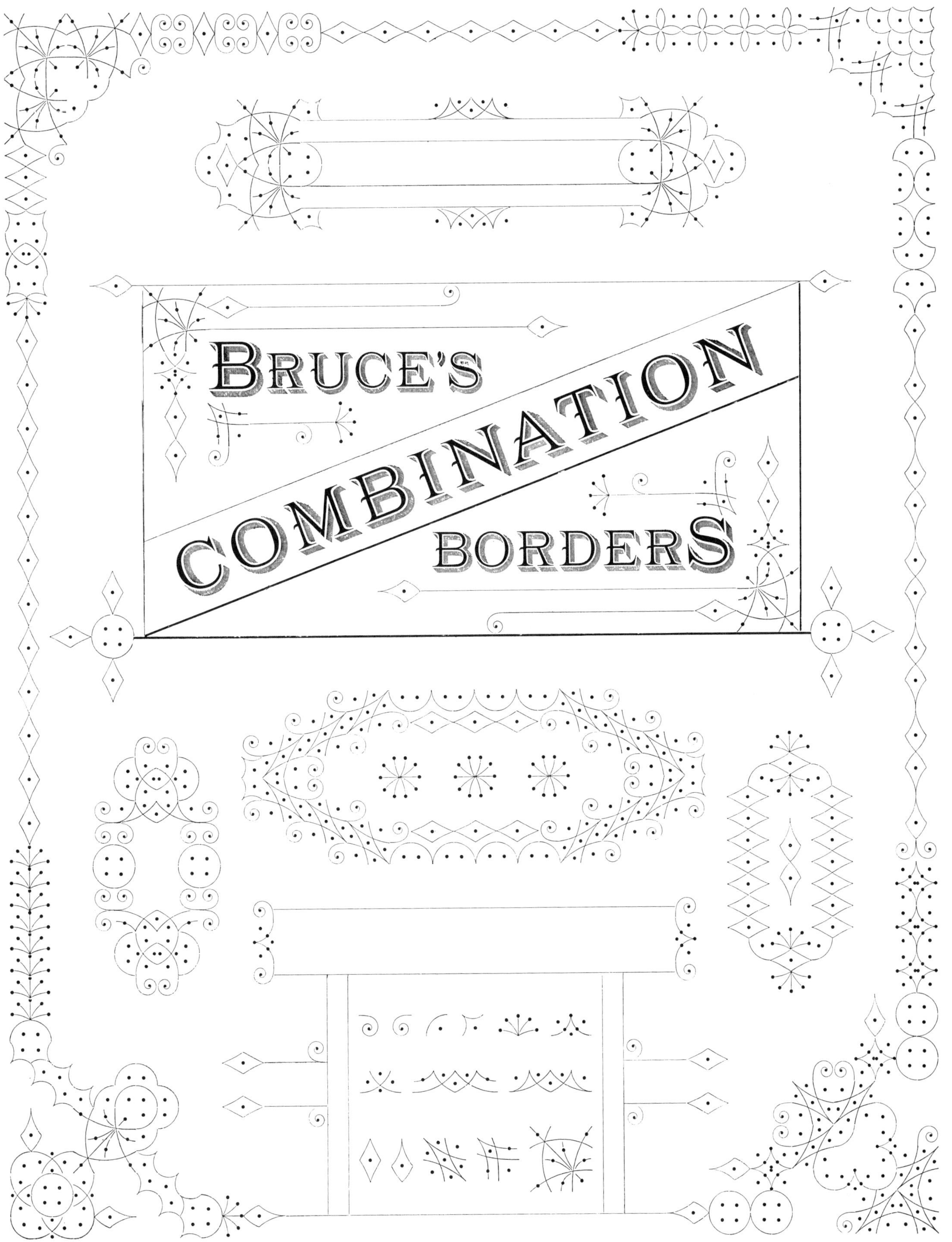
BRUCE'S
COMBINATION
BORDERS

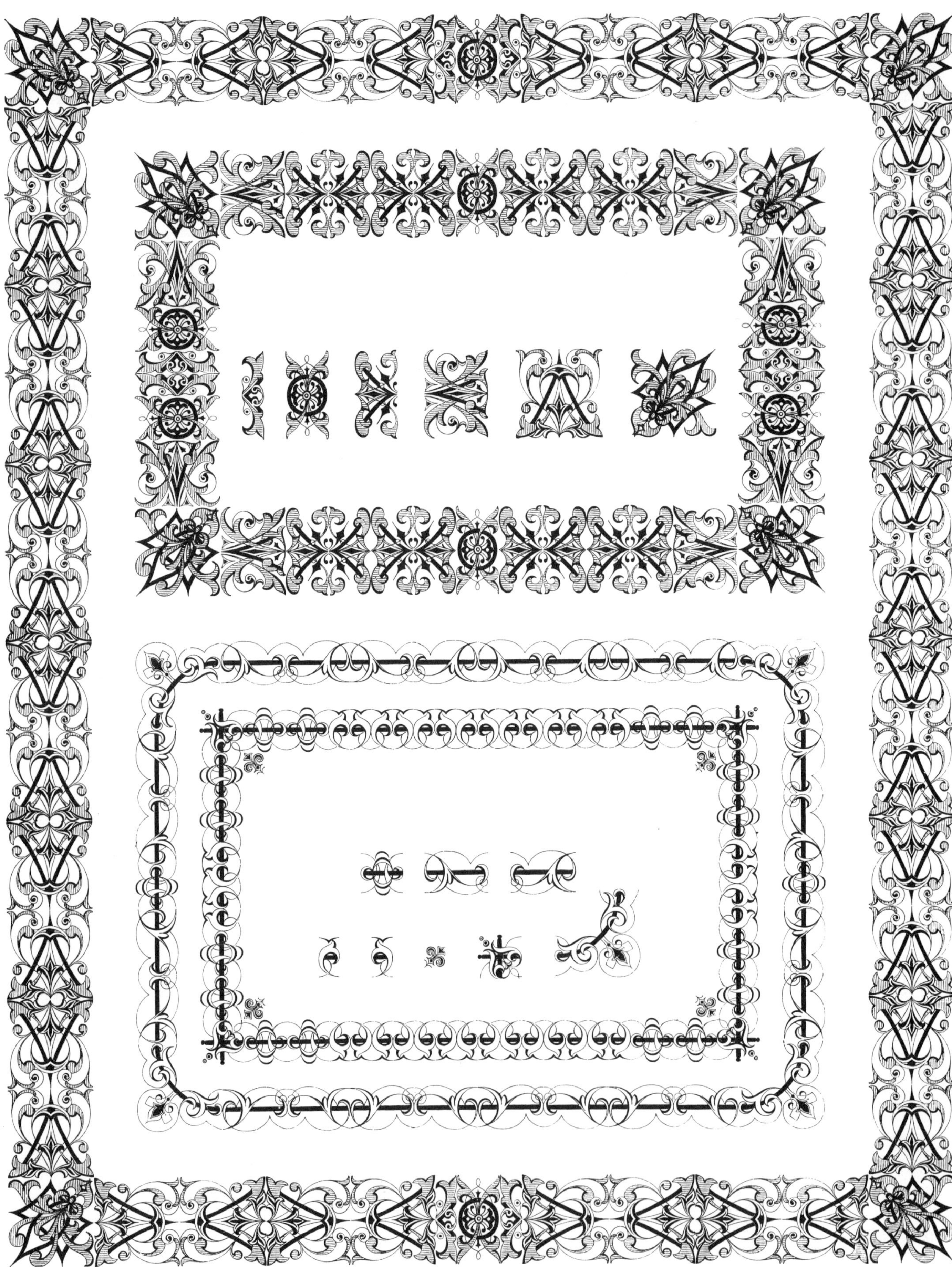

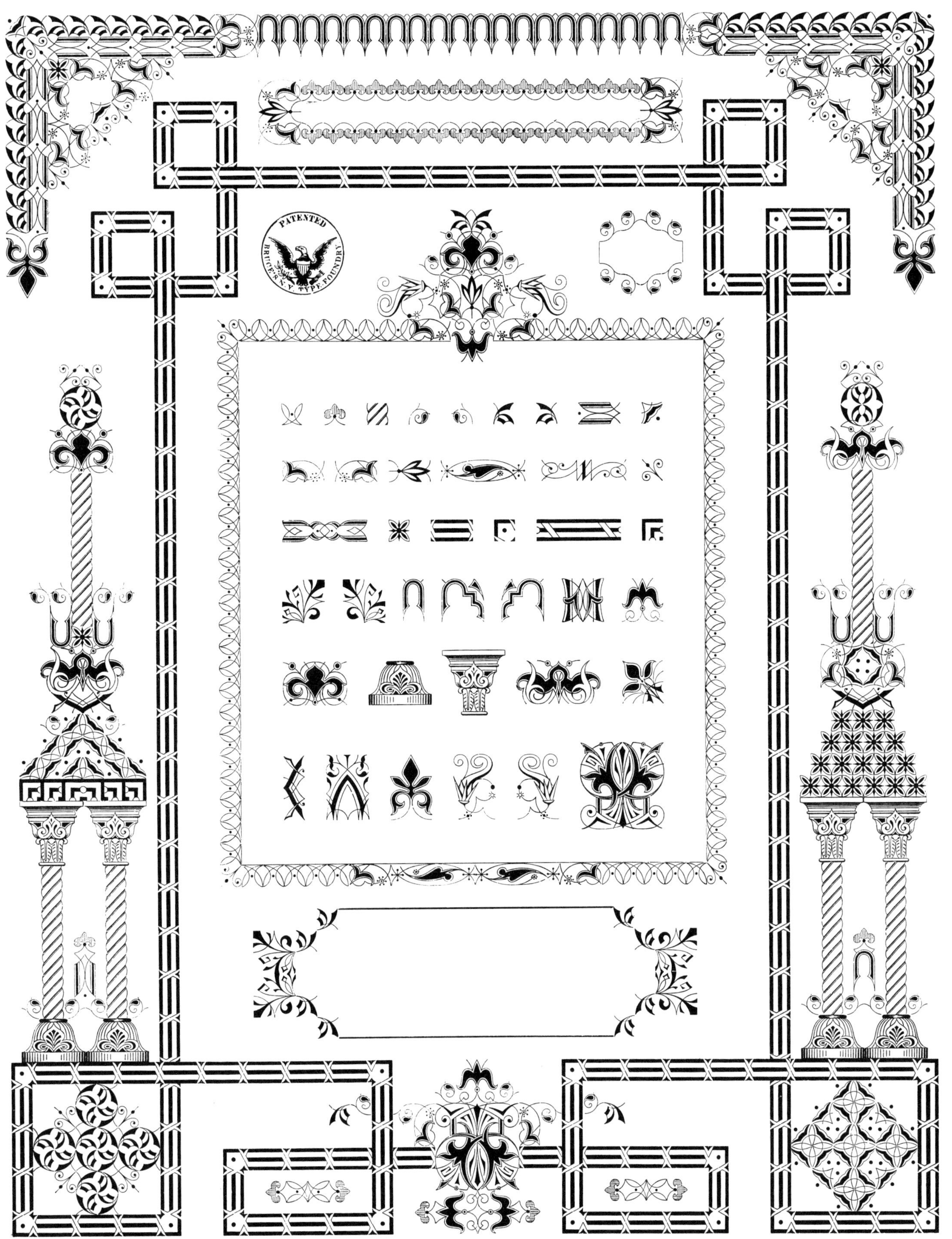
PATENTED
BRUCE'S N.Y. TYPE-FOUNDRY

PATENTED
BRUCE'S N.Y. TYPE FOUNDRY.

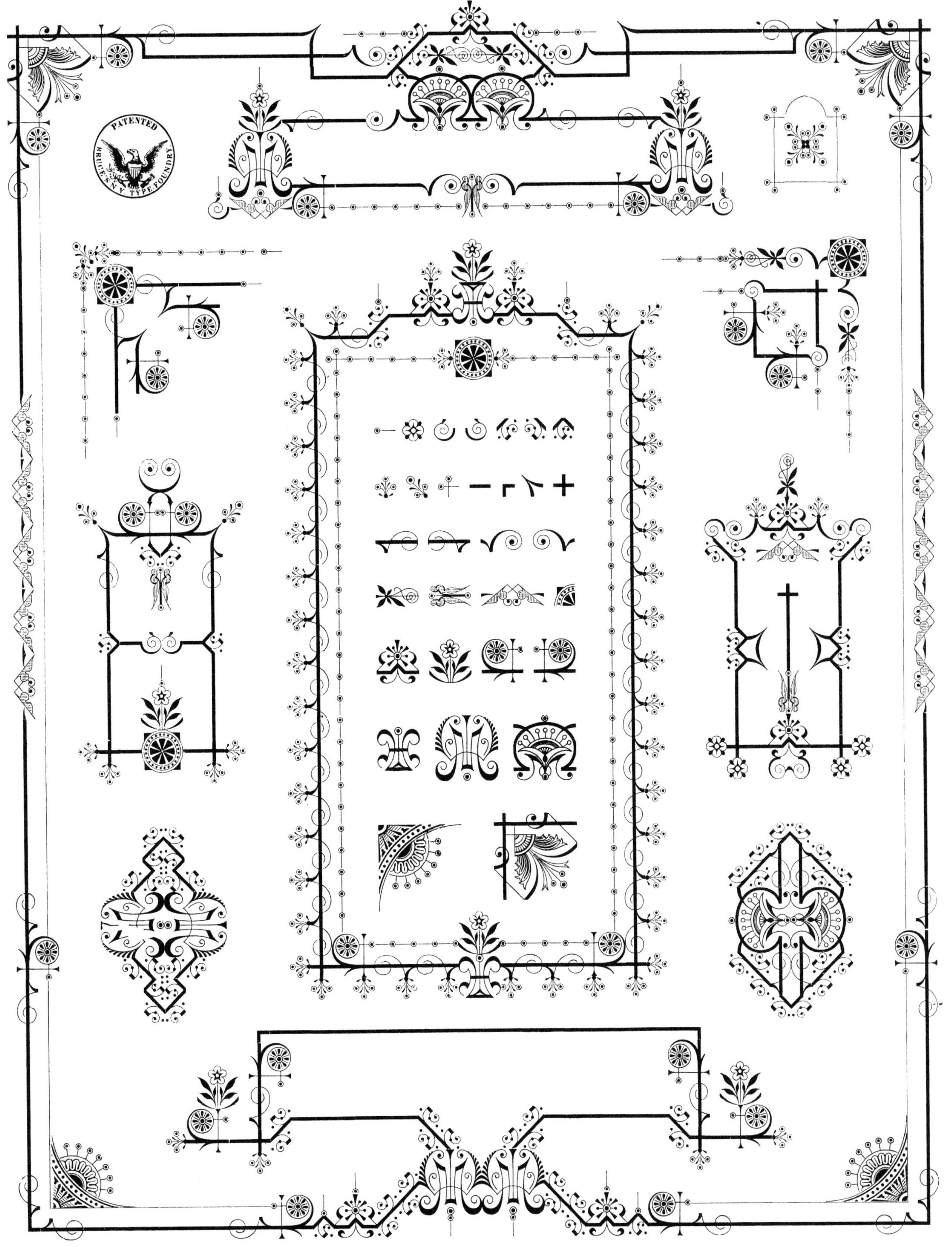
PATENTED
BRUCE'S N Y TYPE FOUNDRY

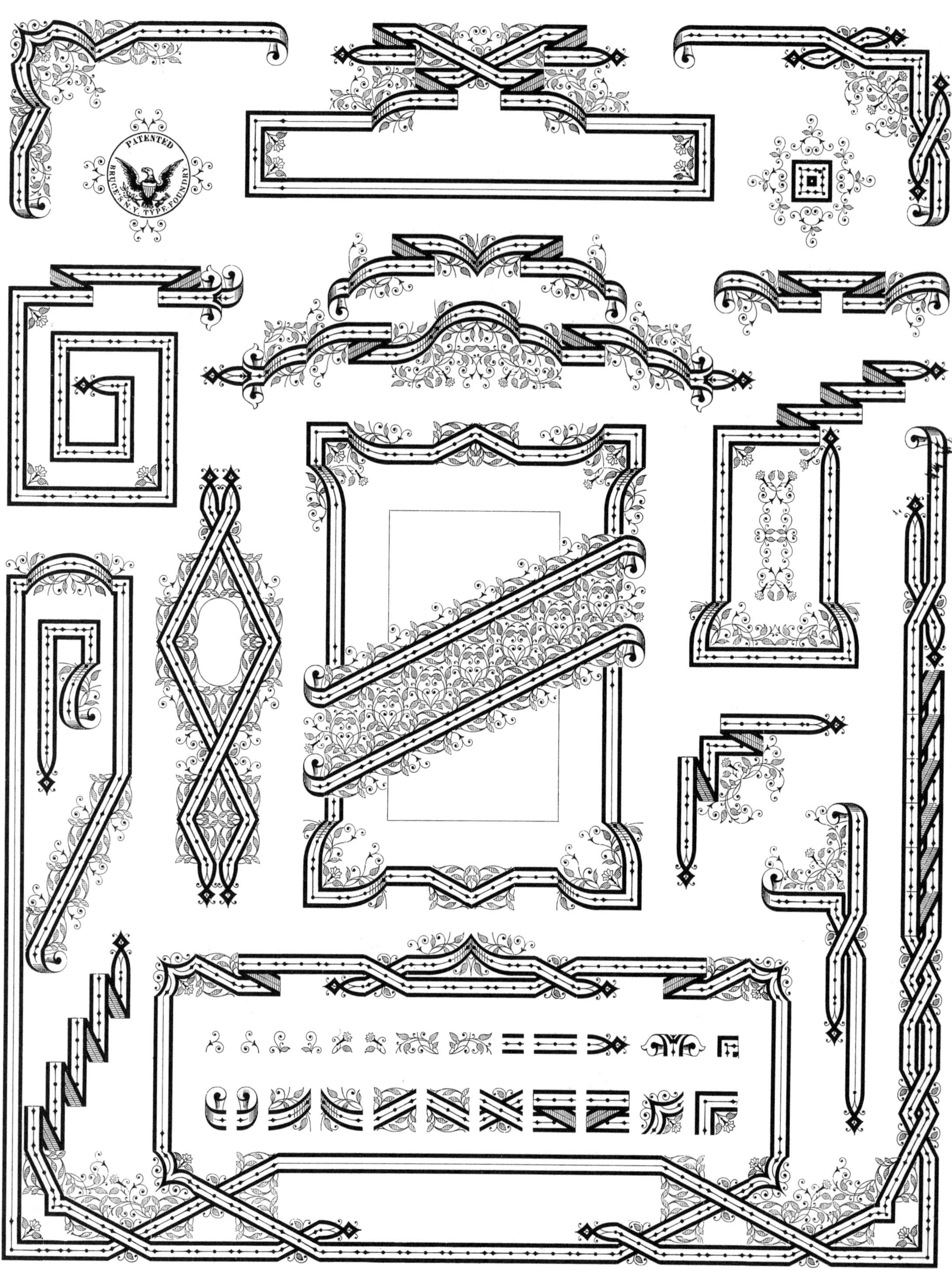
PATENTED
BRUCE'S N.Y. TYPE FOUNDRY

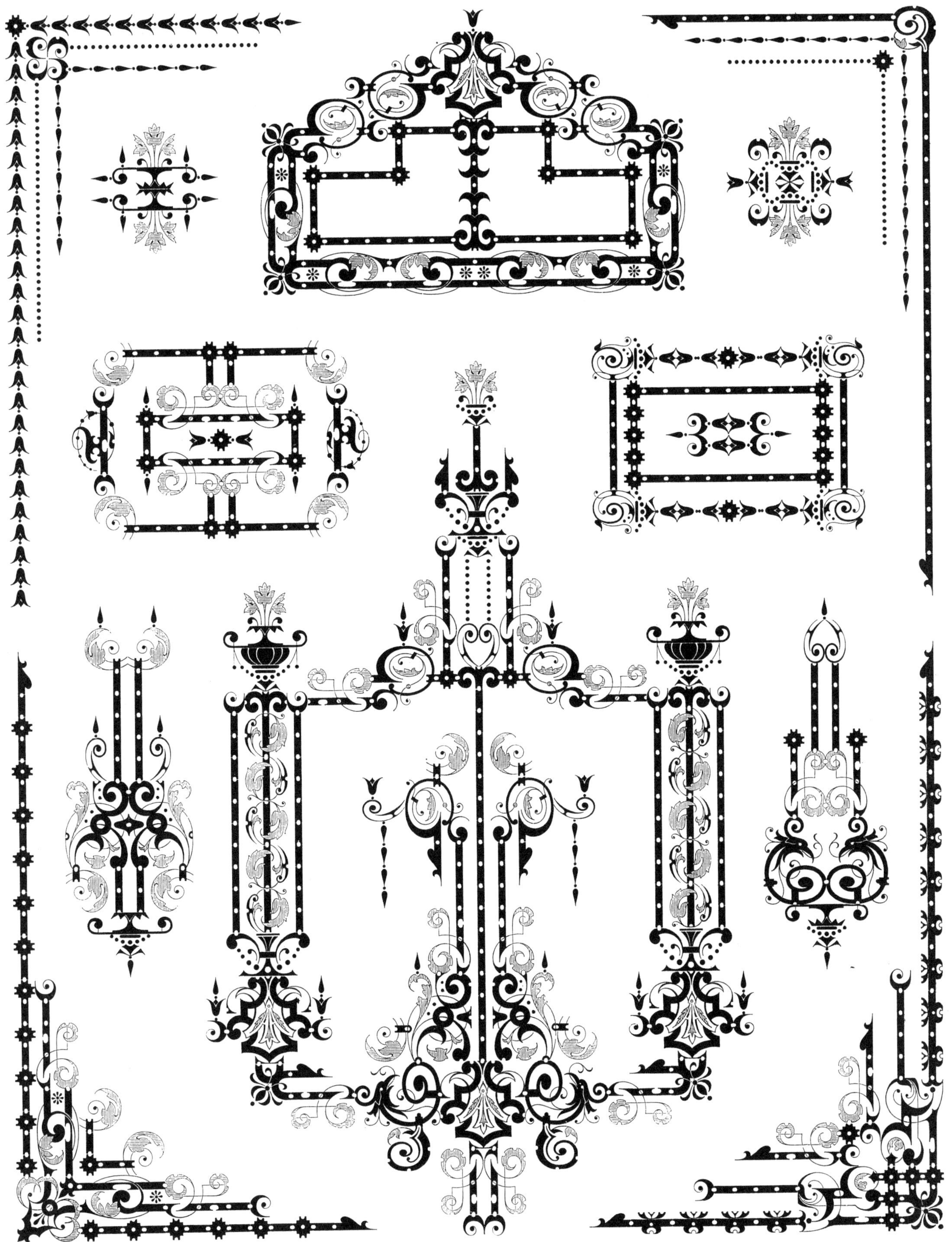

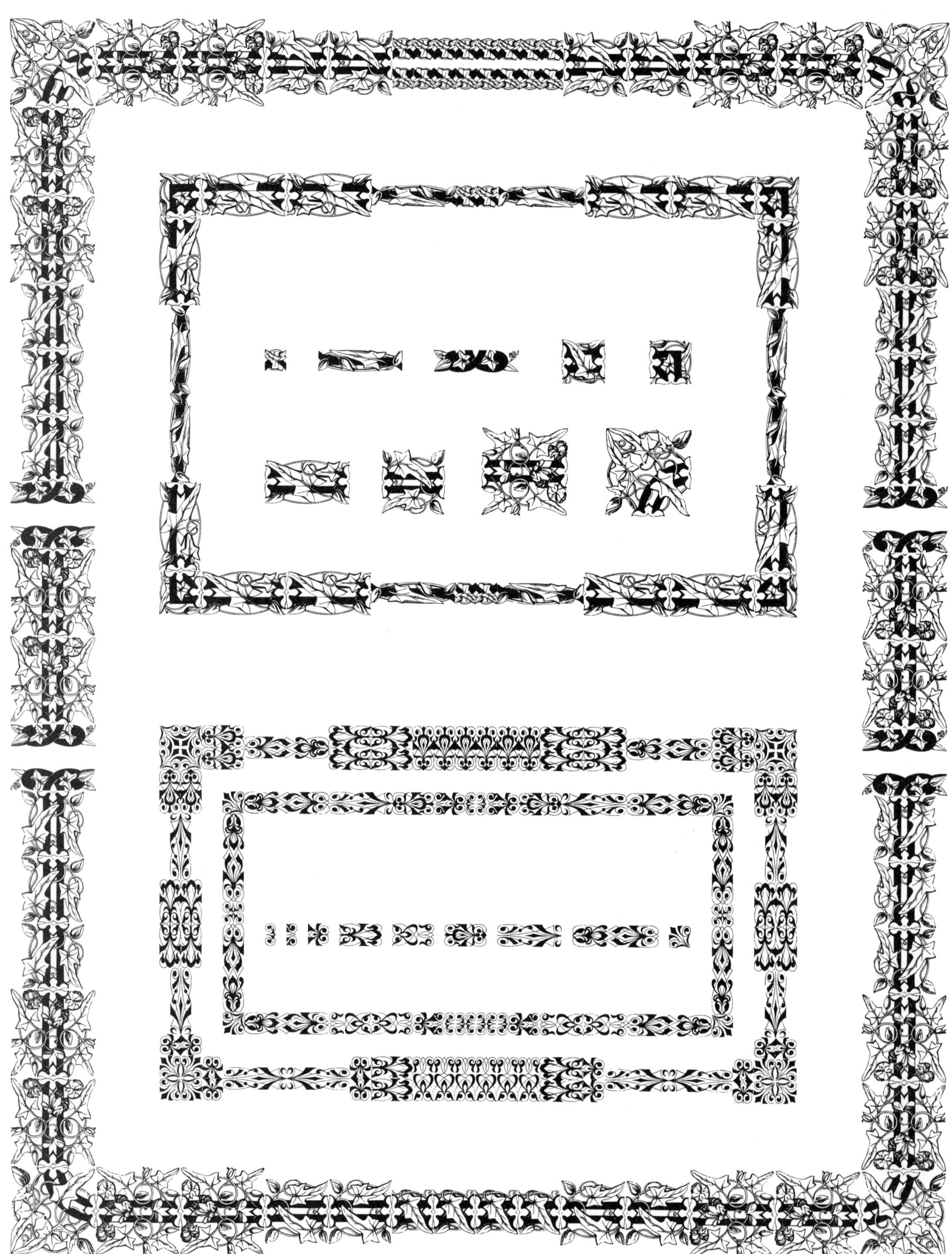

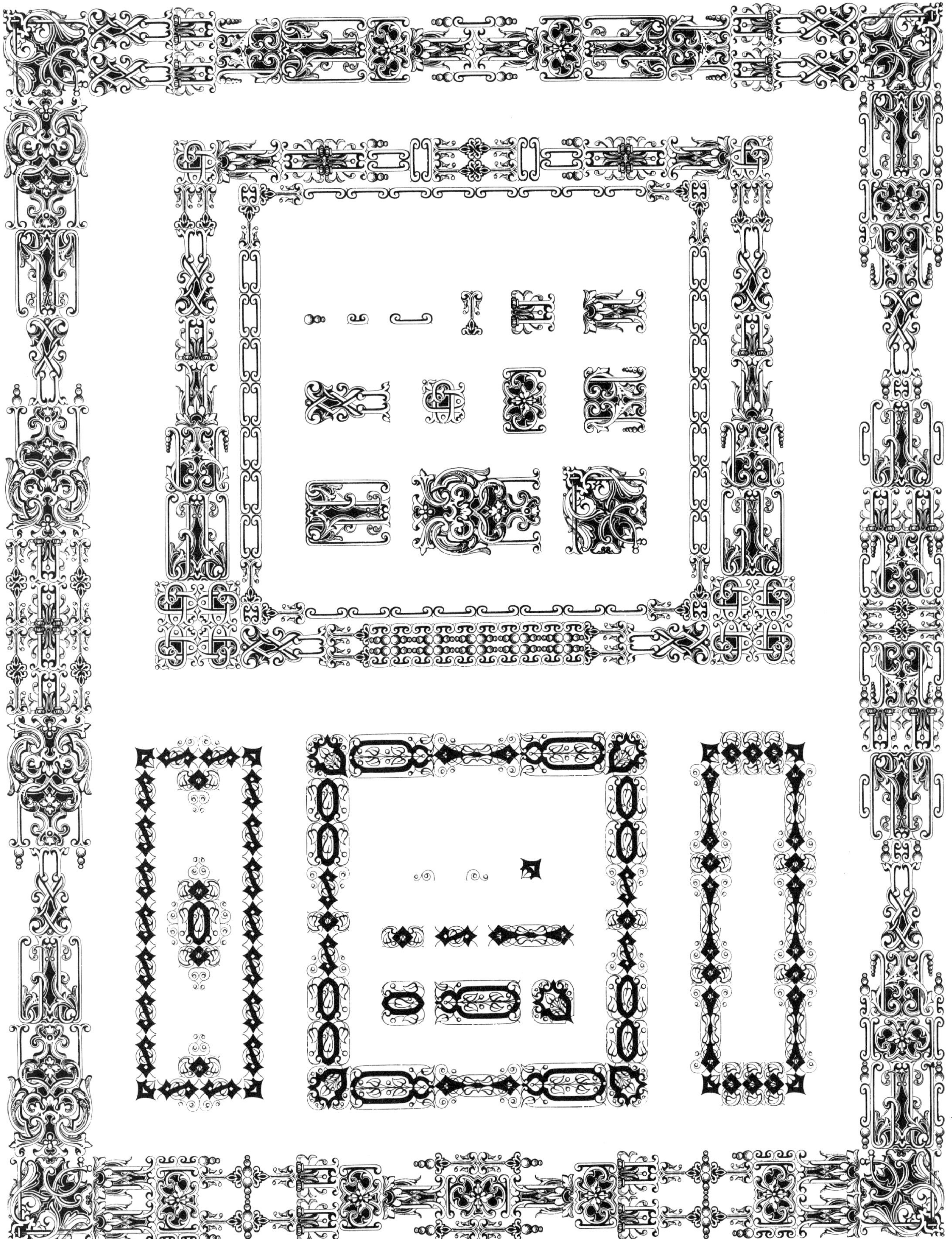

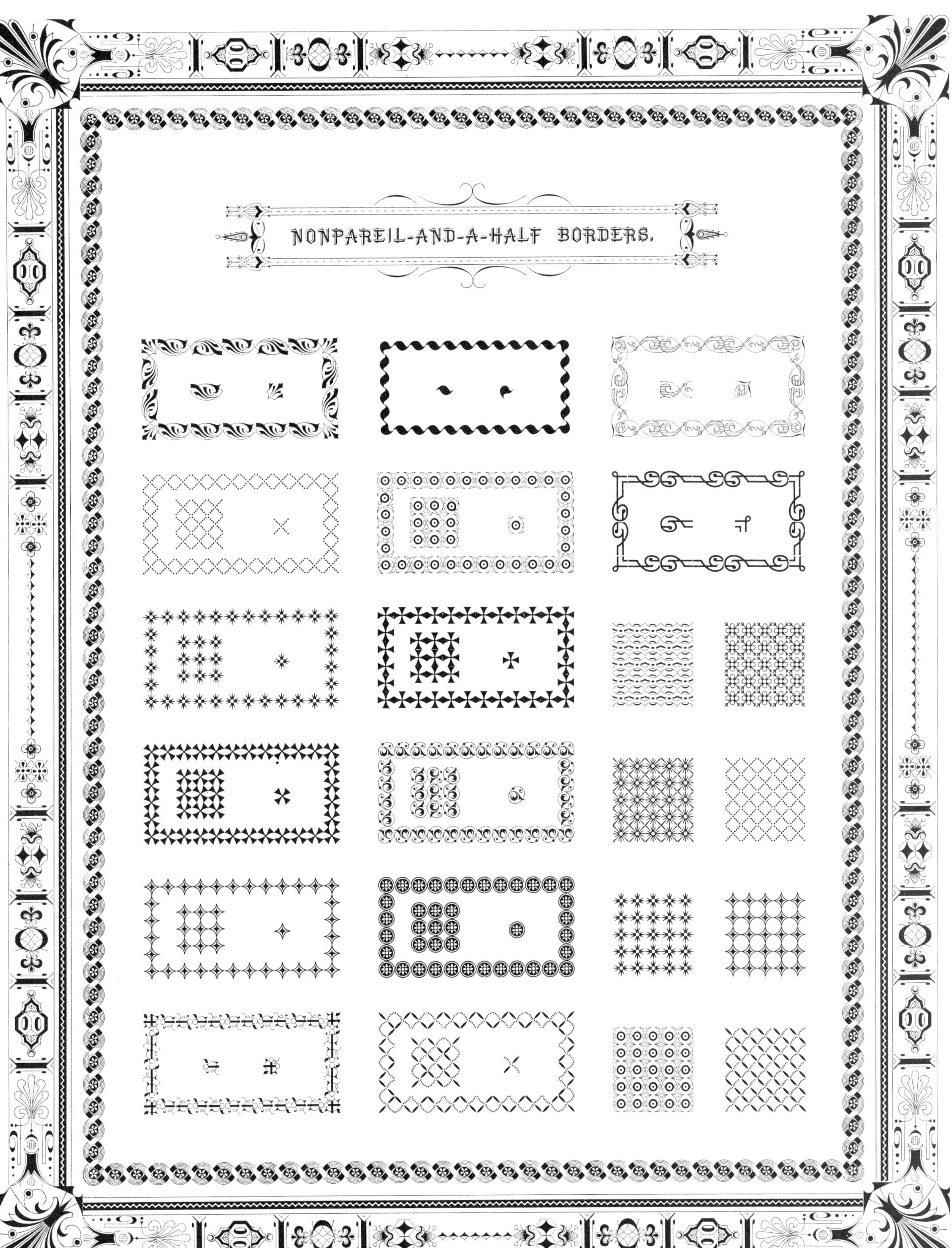
NONPAREIL-AND-A-HALF BORDERS.

BRUCE'S
BORDERS.

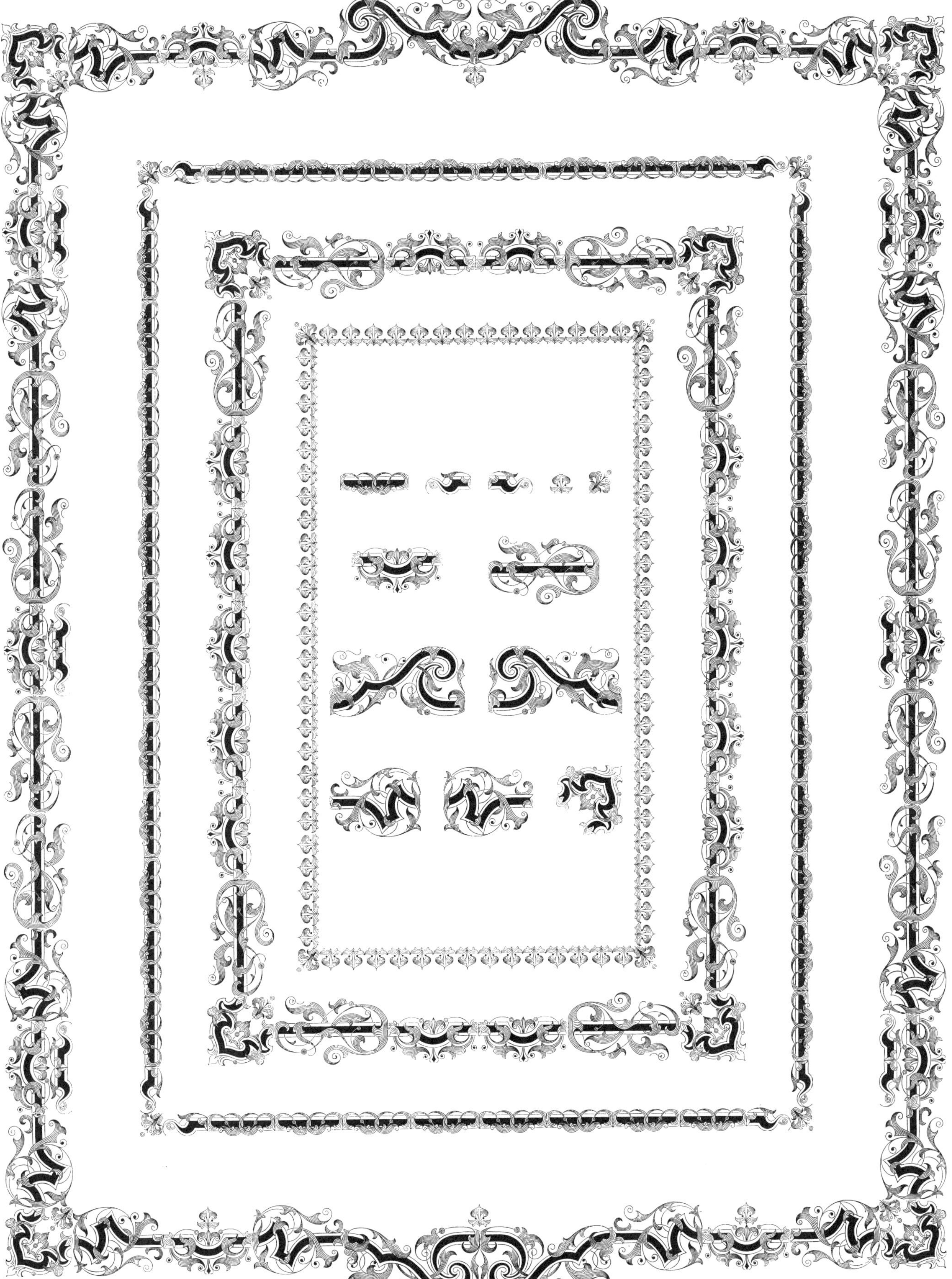

NONPAREIL-AND-A-HALF BORDERS.

NONPAREIL-AND-A-HALF BORDERS.

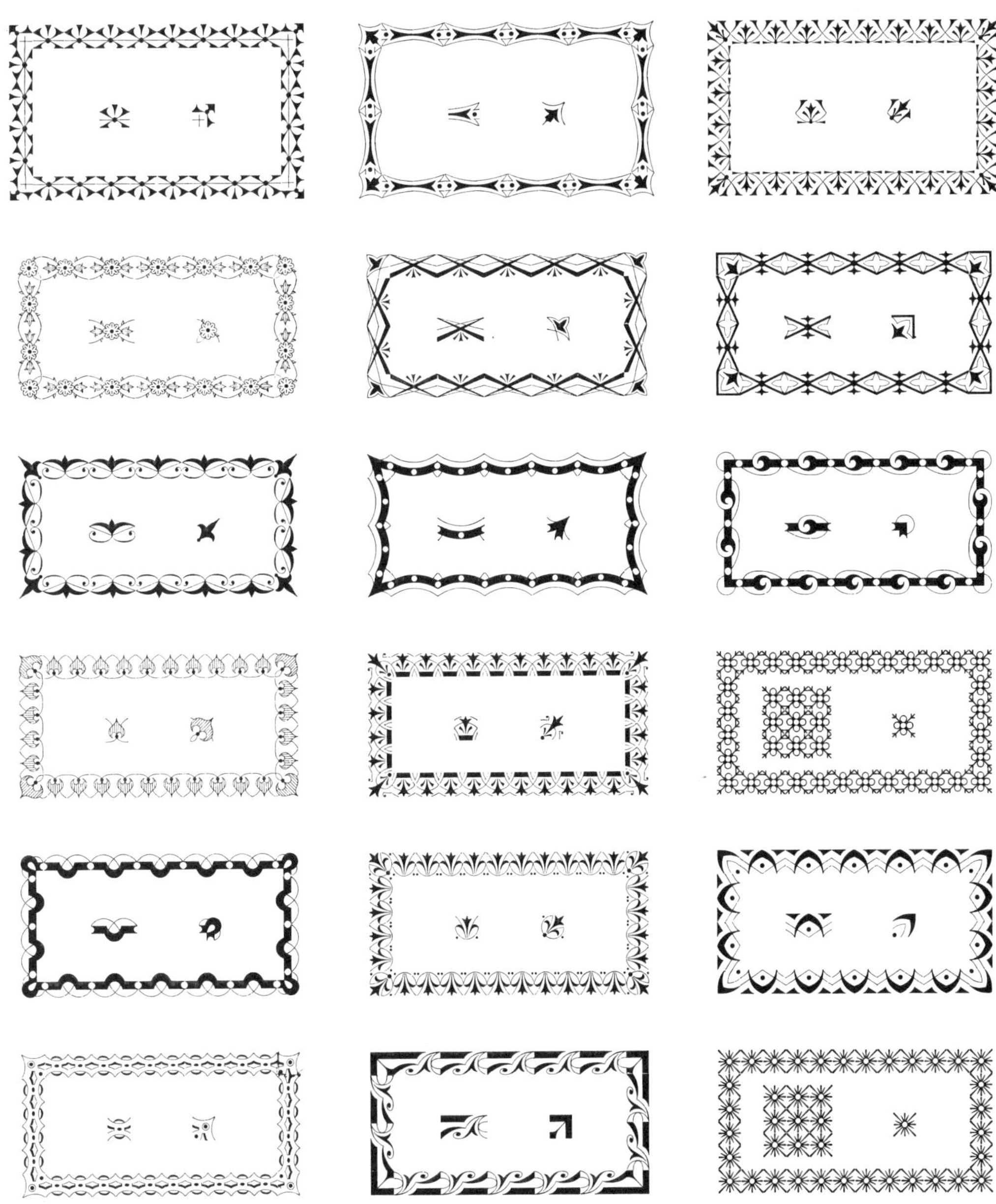

NONPAREIL BORDERS.

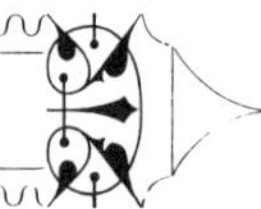

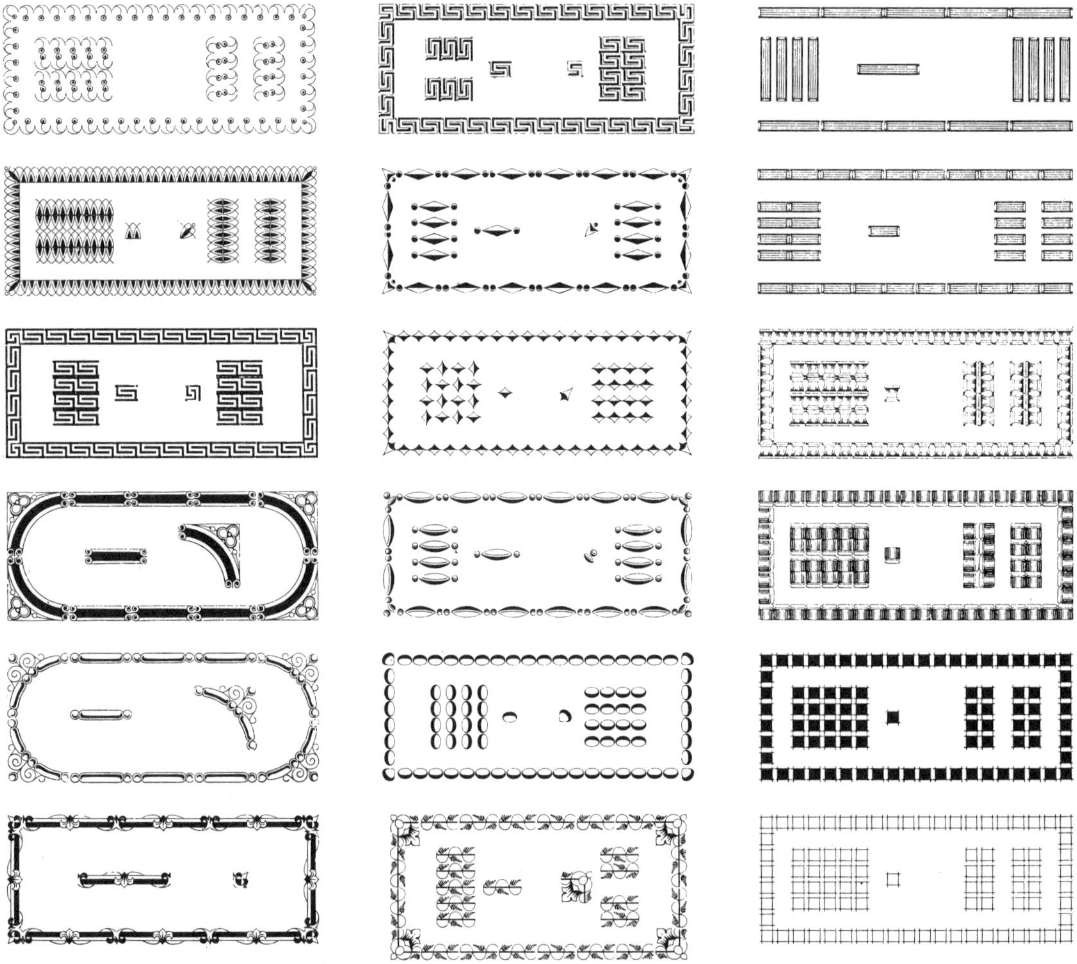

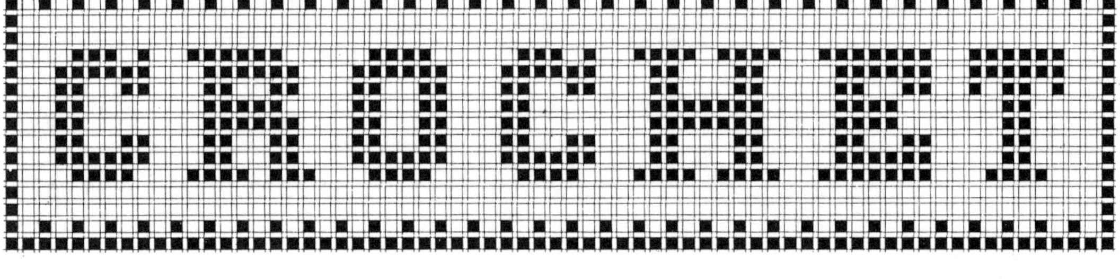

CROCHET

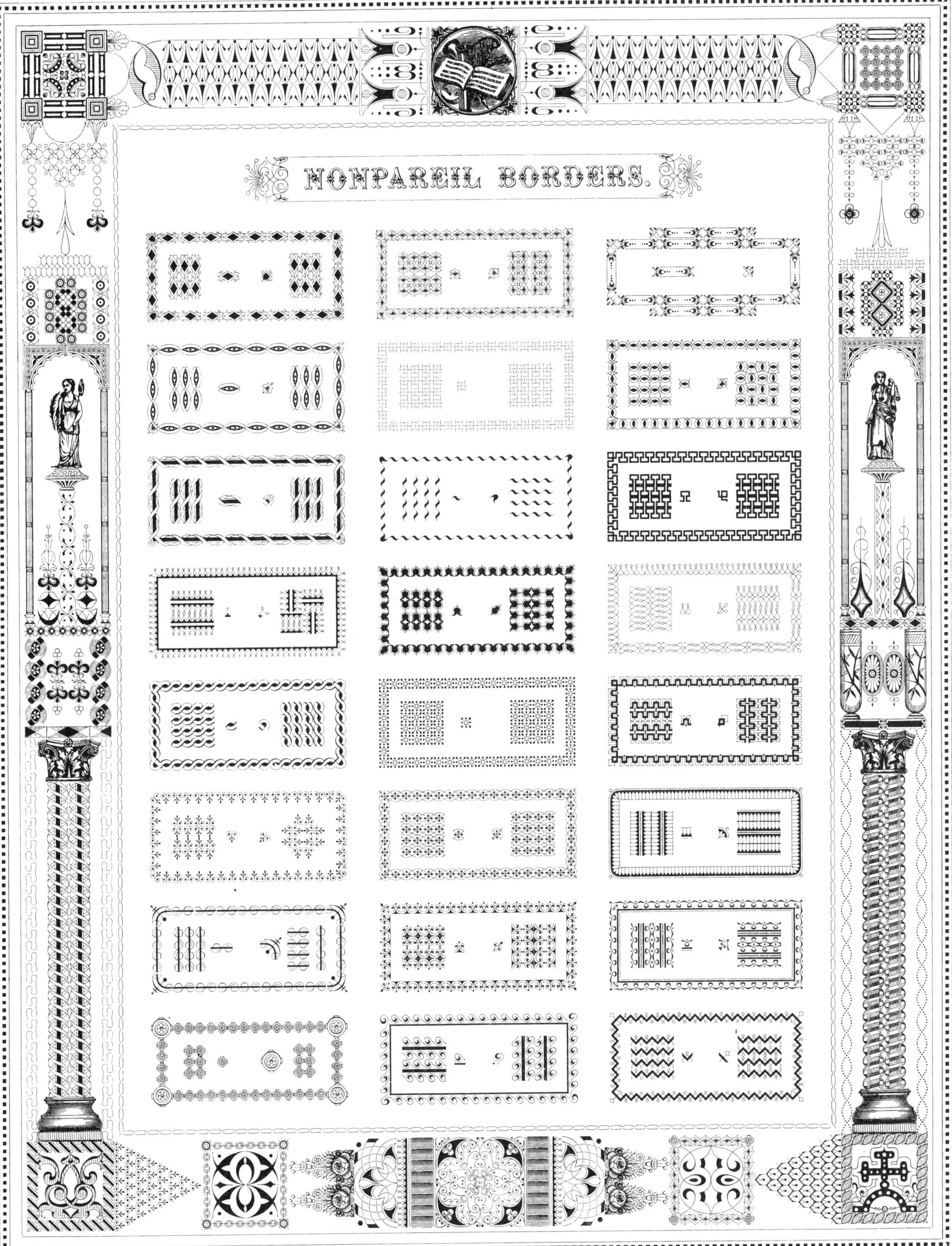
NONPAREIL BORDERS.

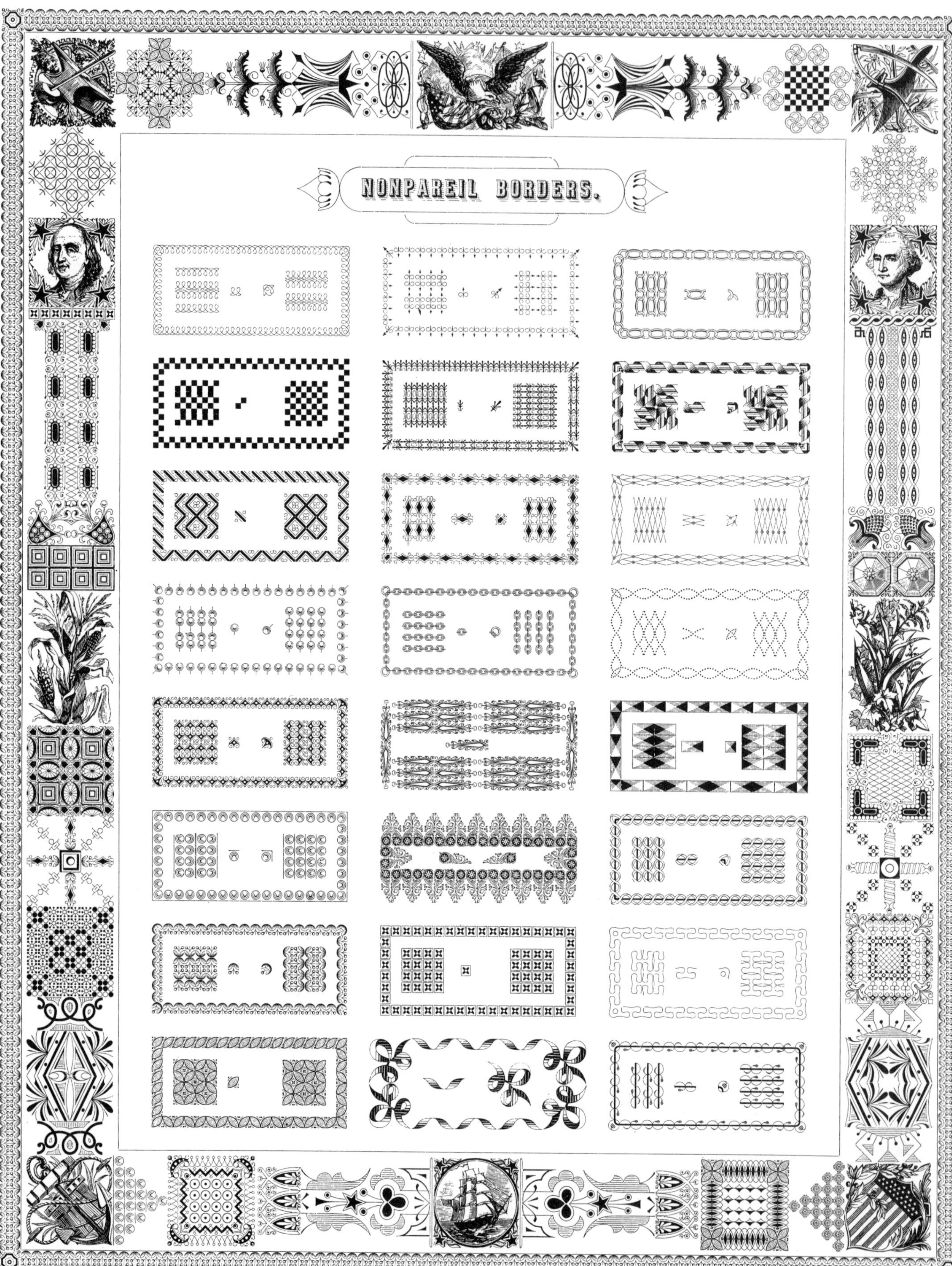
NONPAREIL BORDERS.

NONPAREIL BORDERS.

NONPAREIL-AND-A-HALF BORDERS.

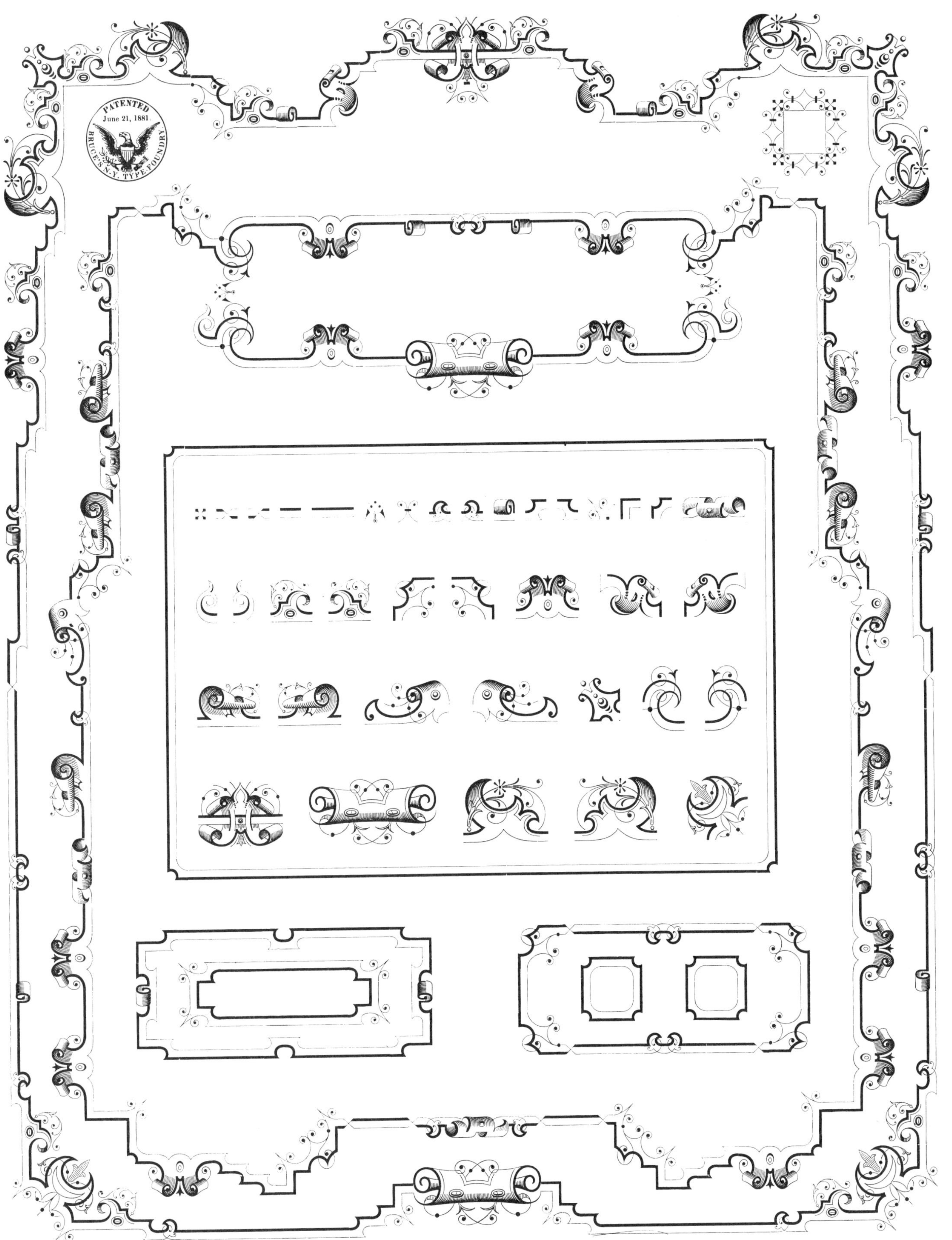
PATENTED
June 21, 1881.
BRUCE'S N.Y. TYPE-FOUNDRY

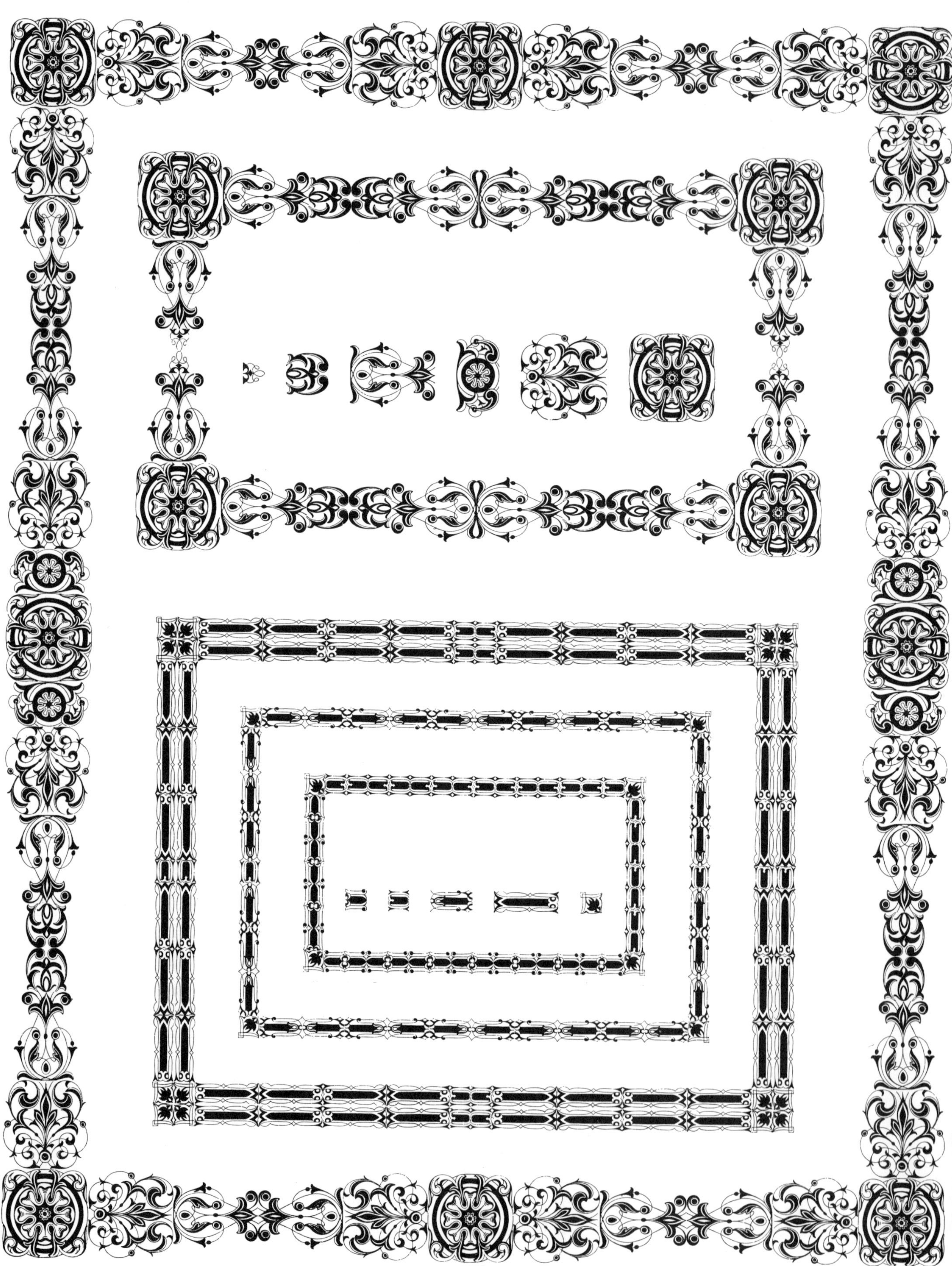

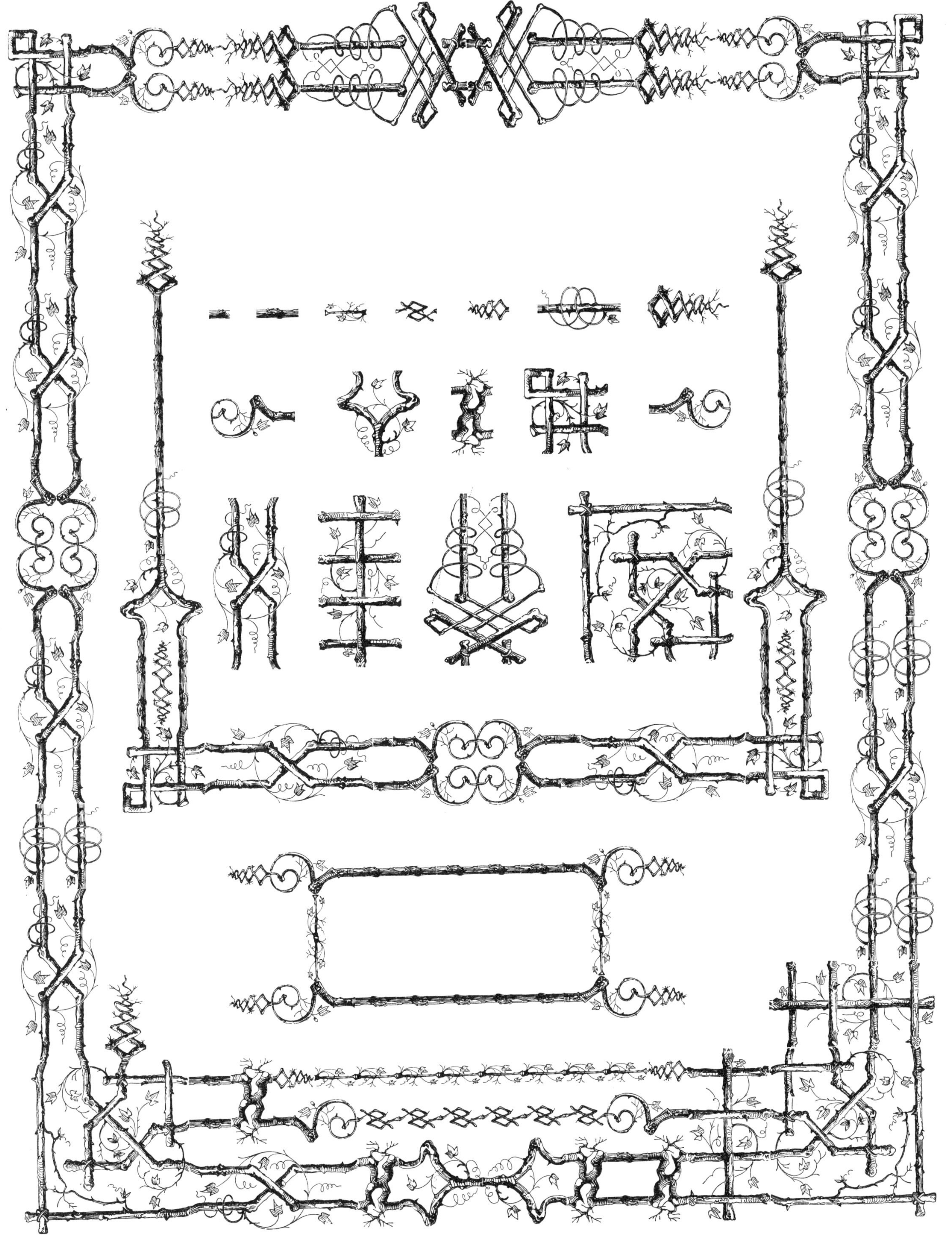

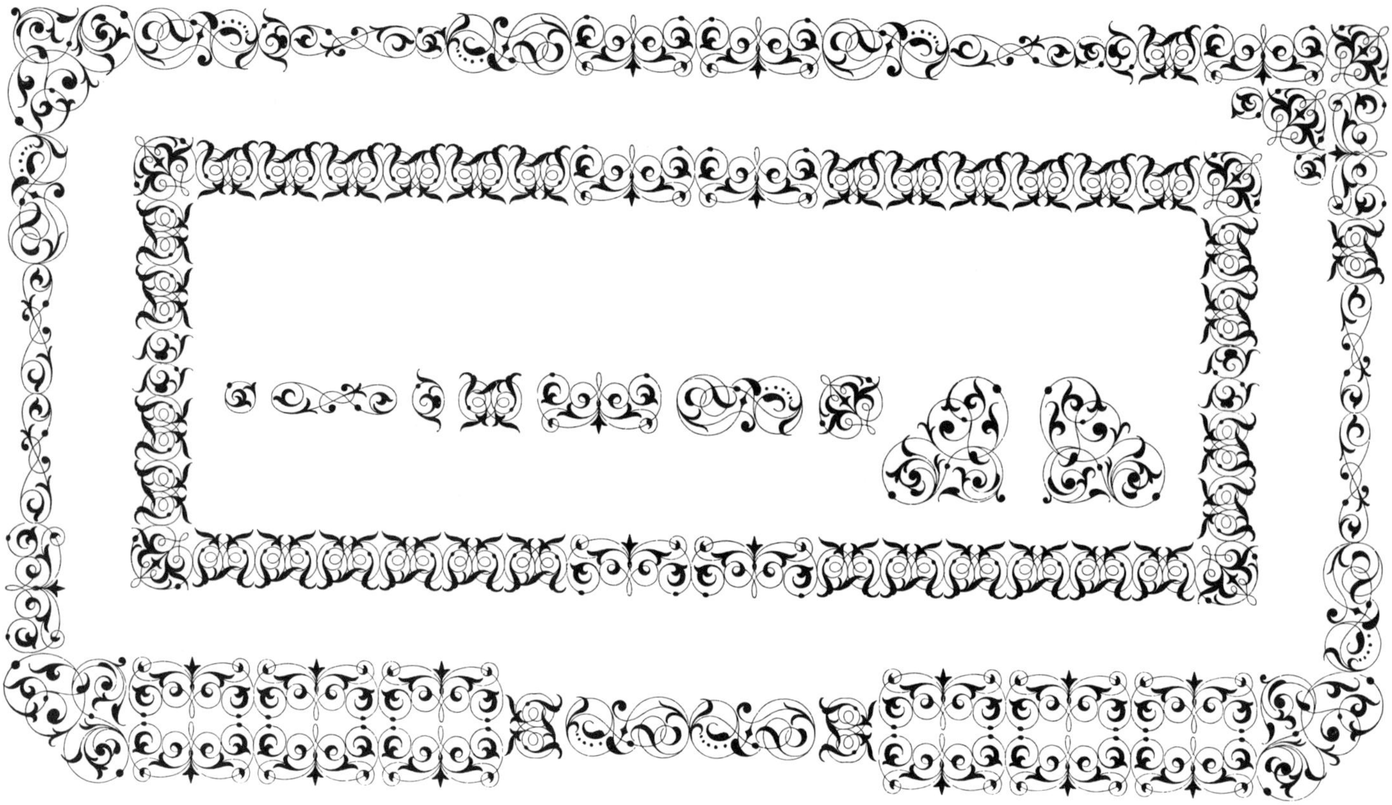

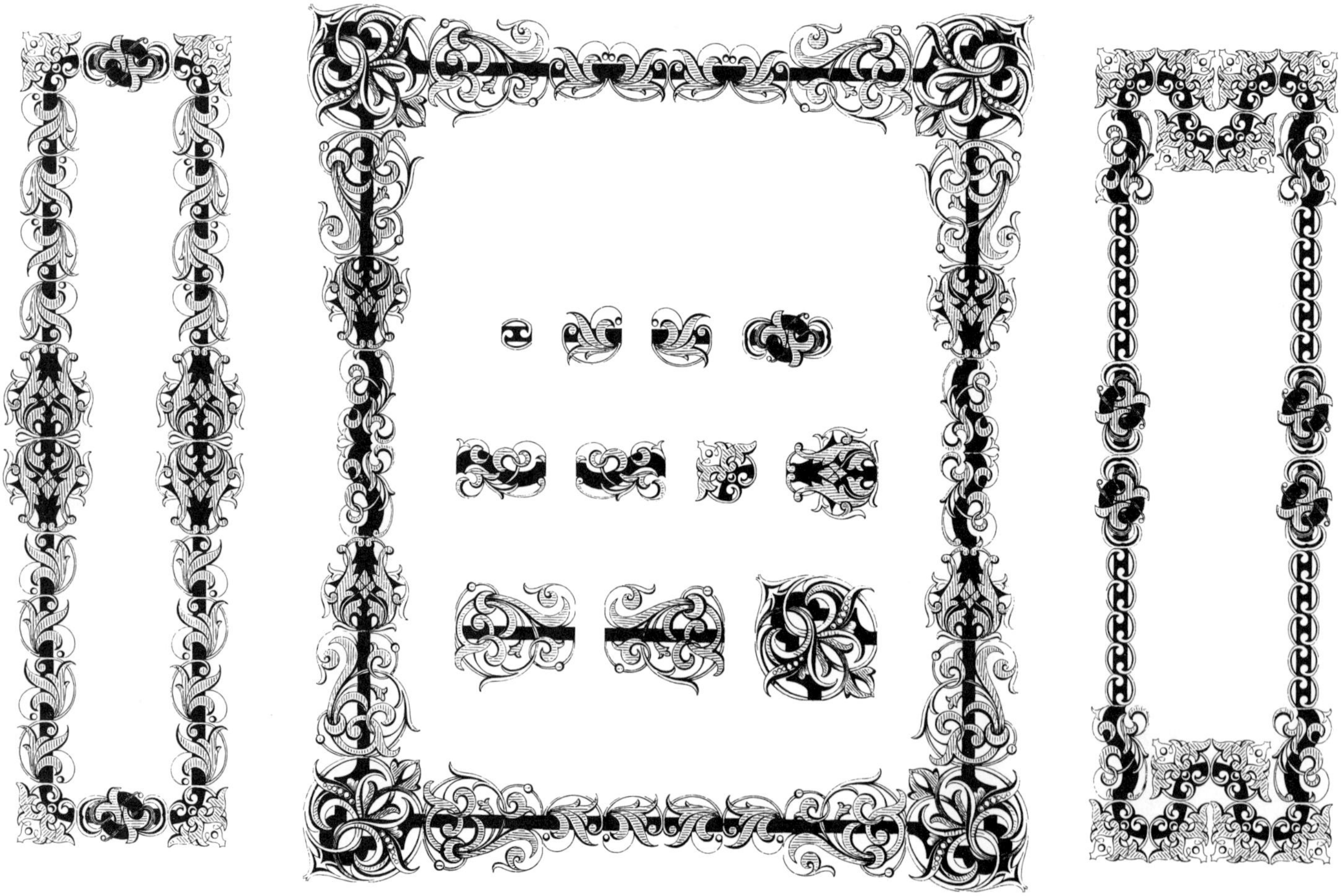

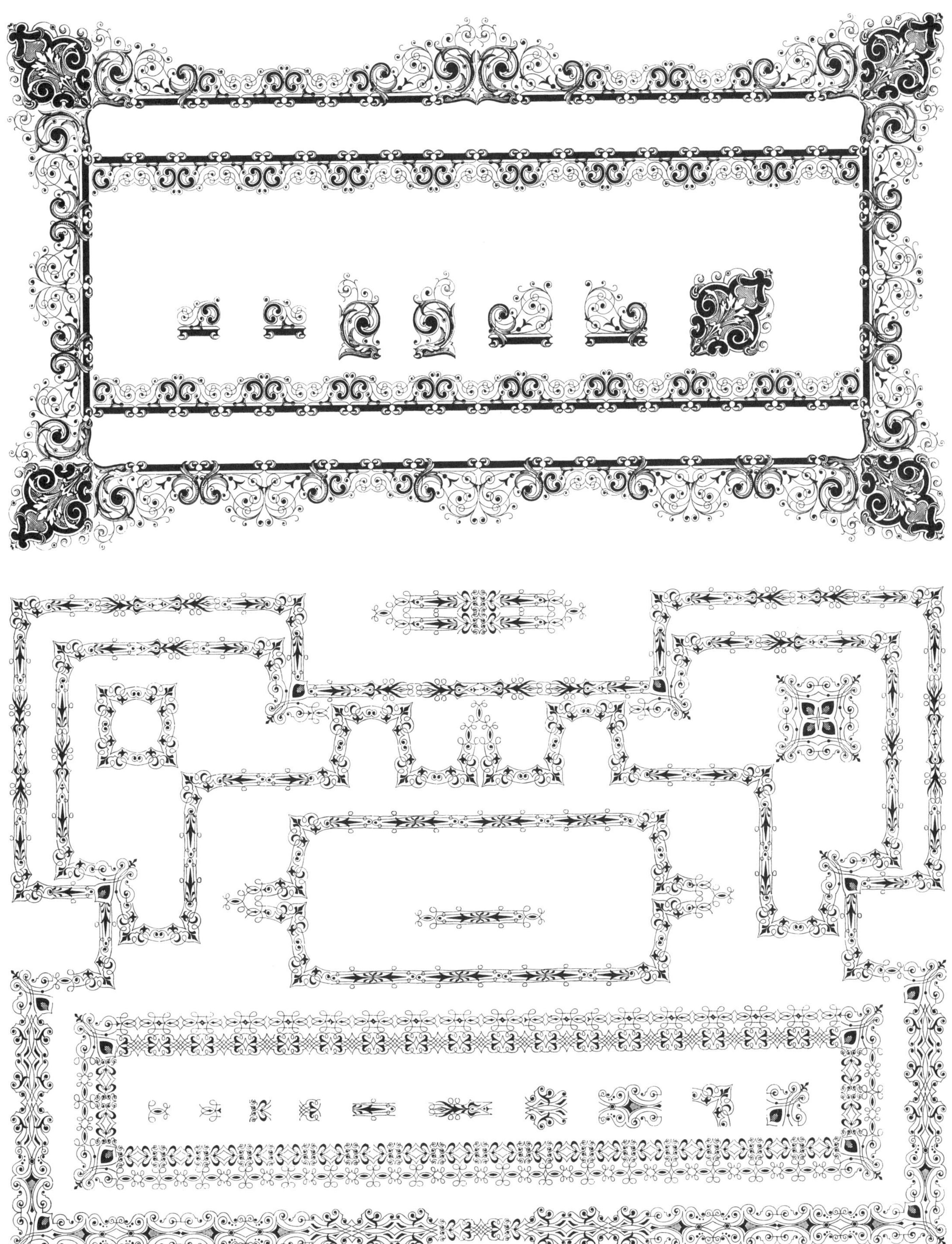

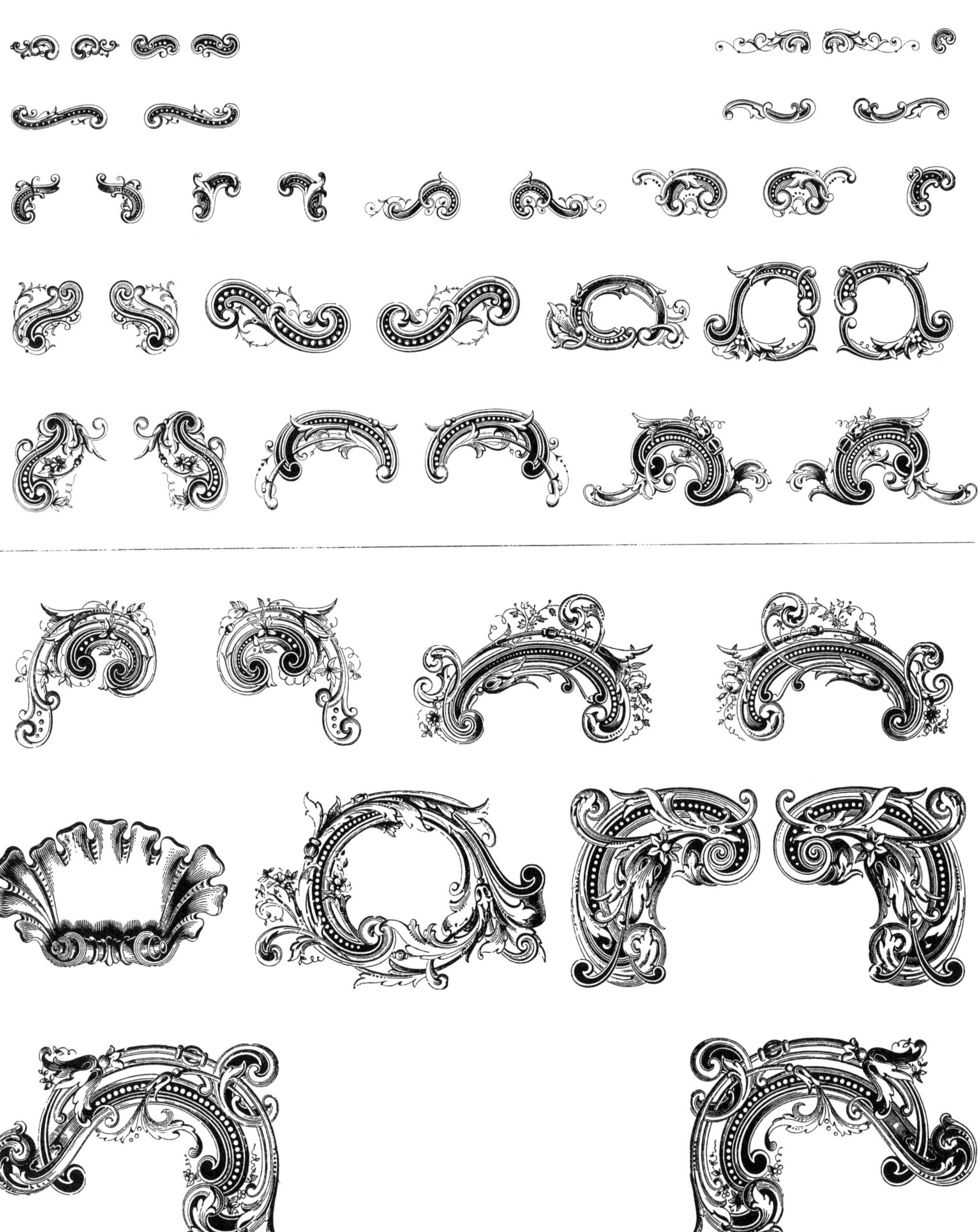

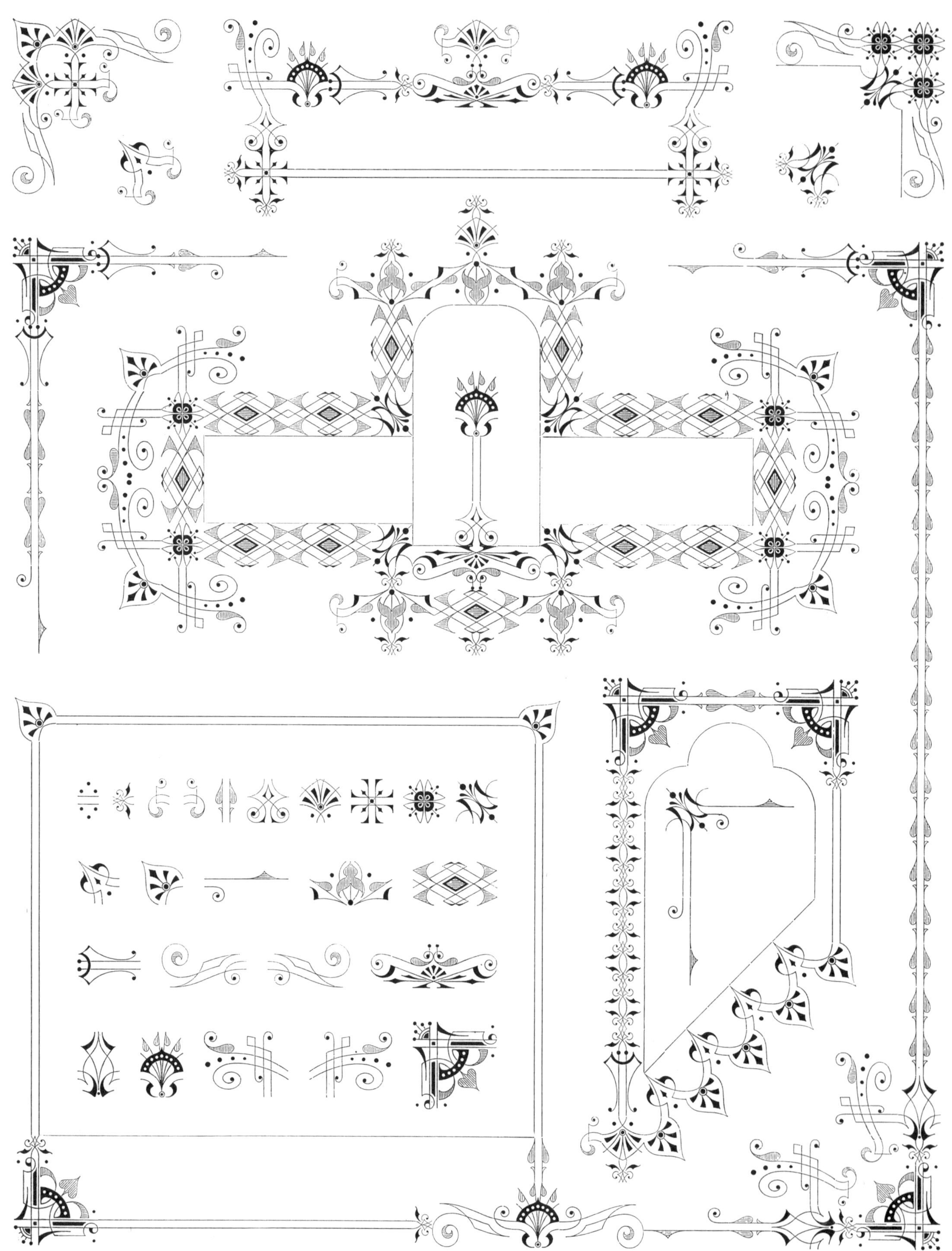

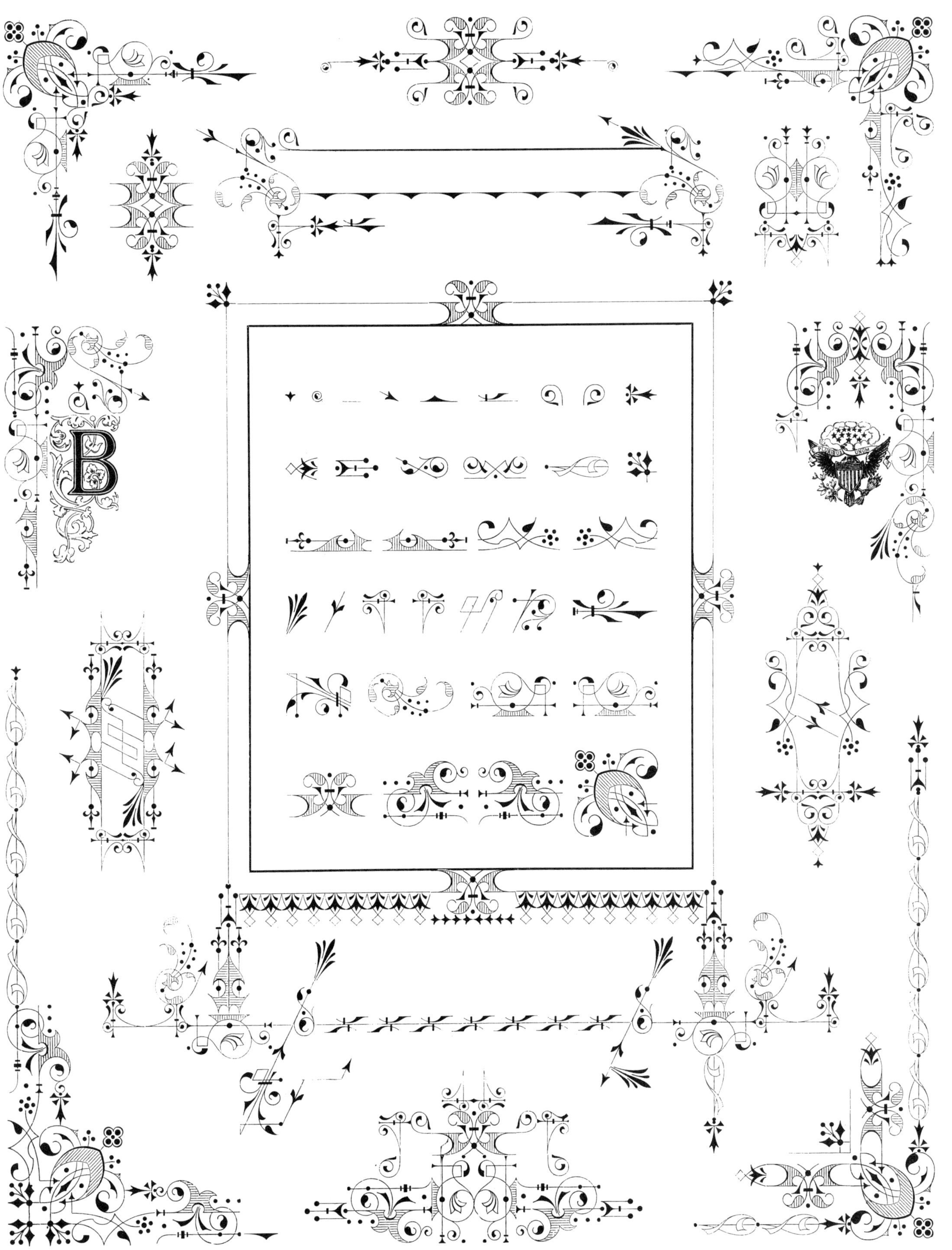

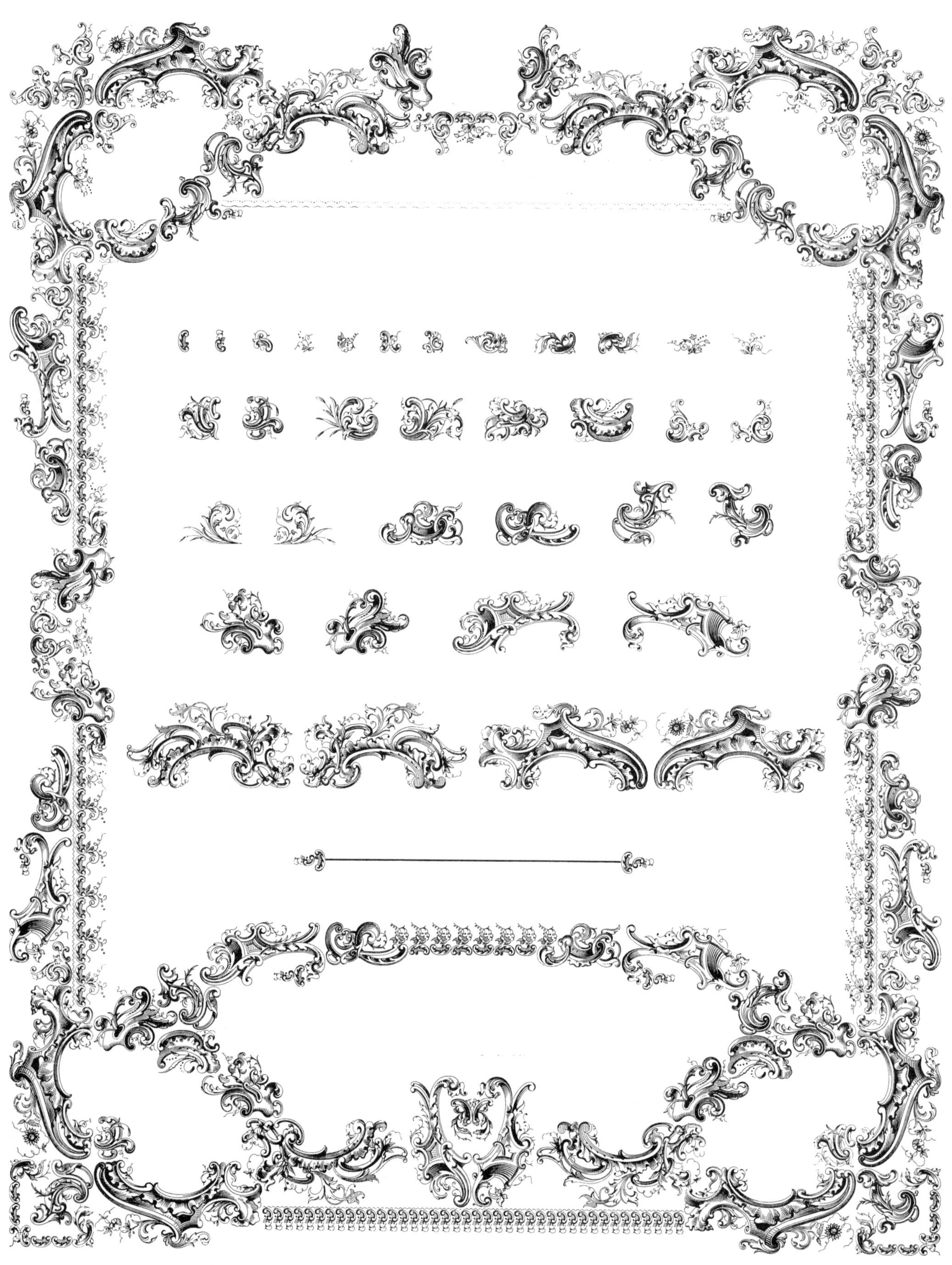

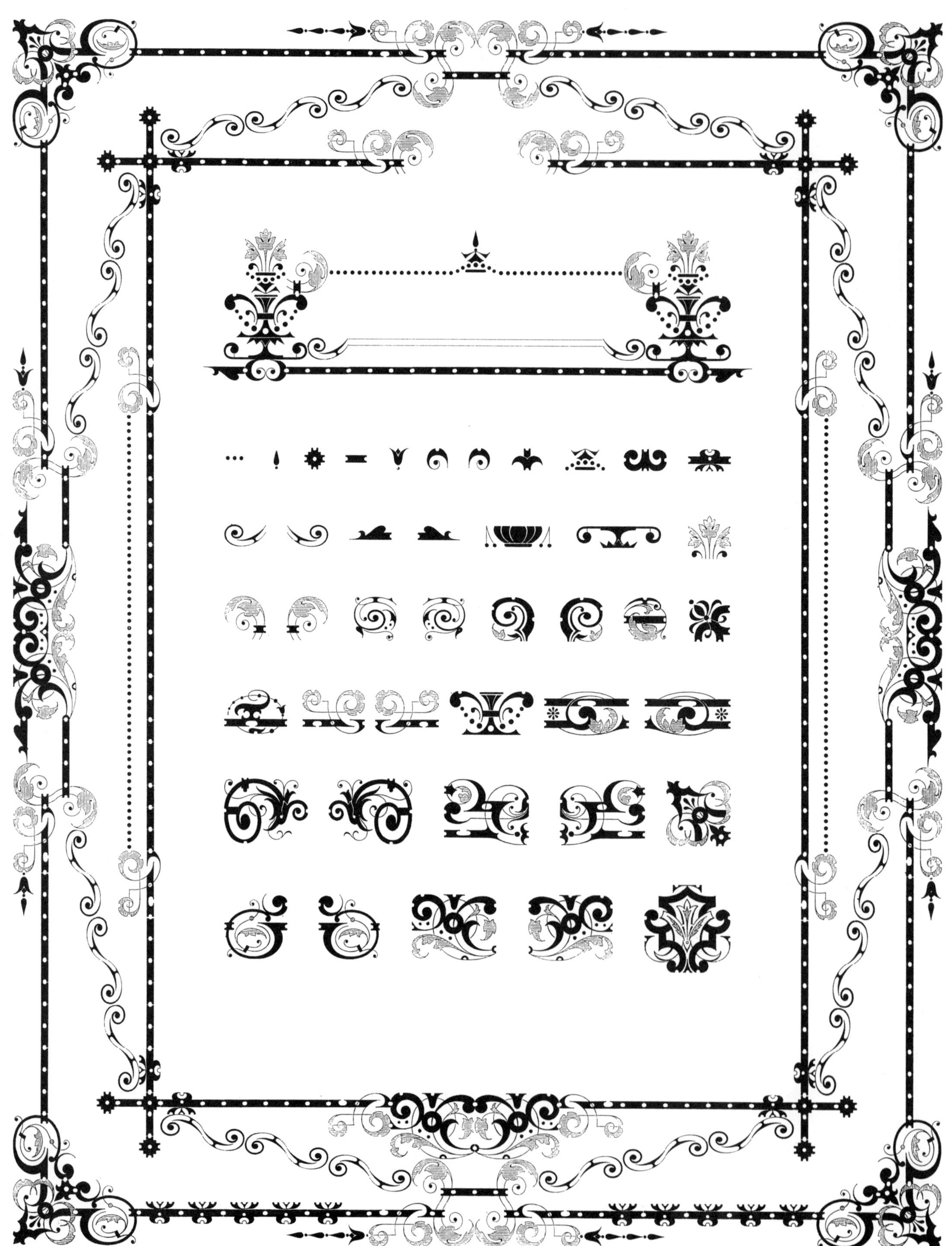

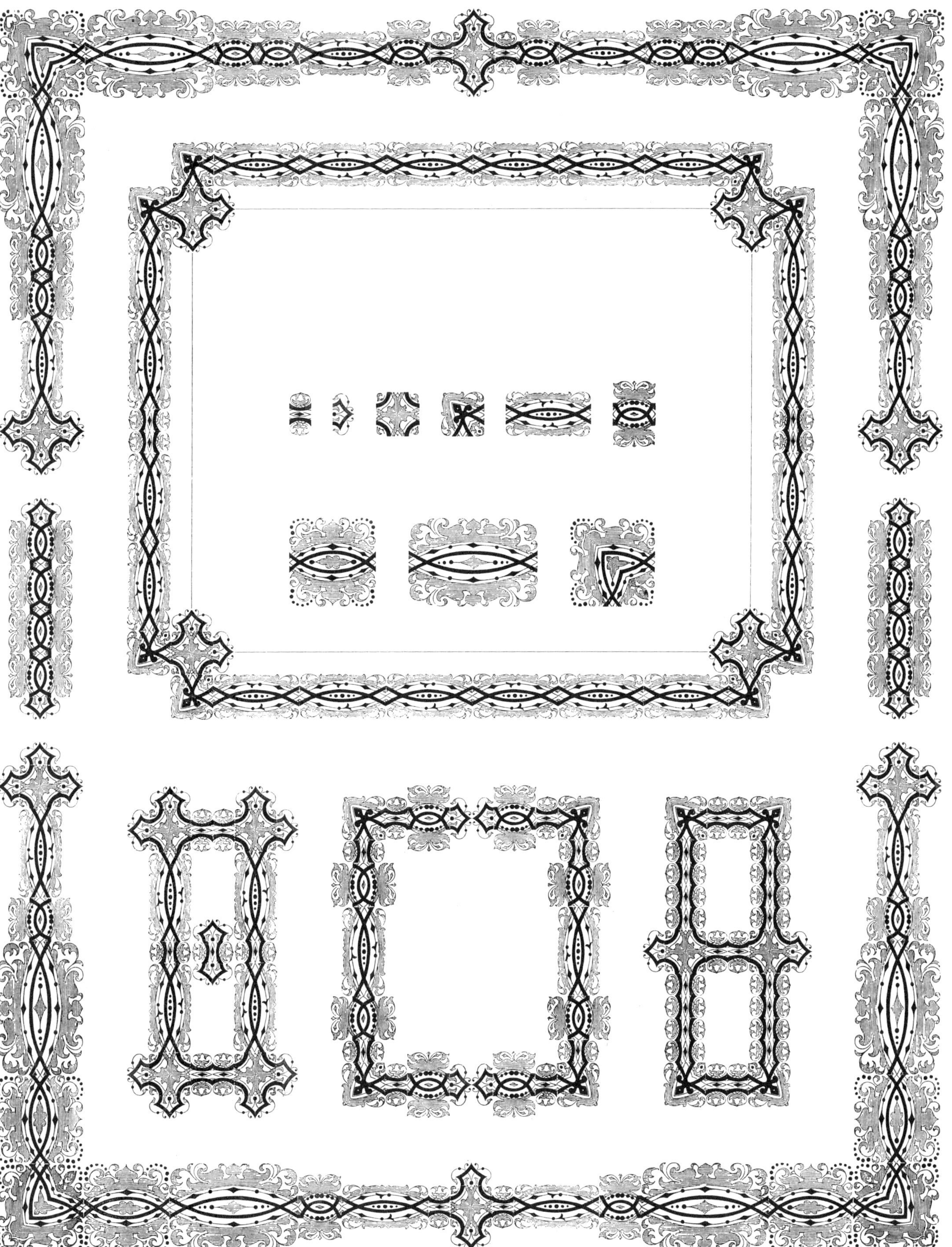

Received of
or Bearer,

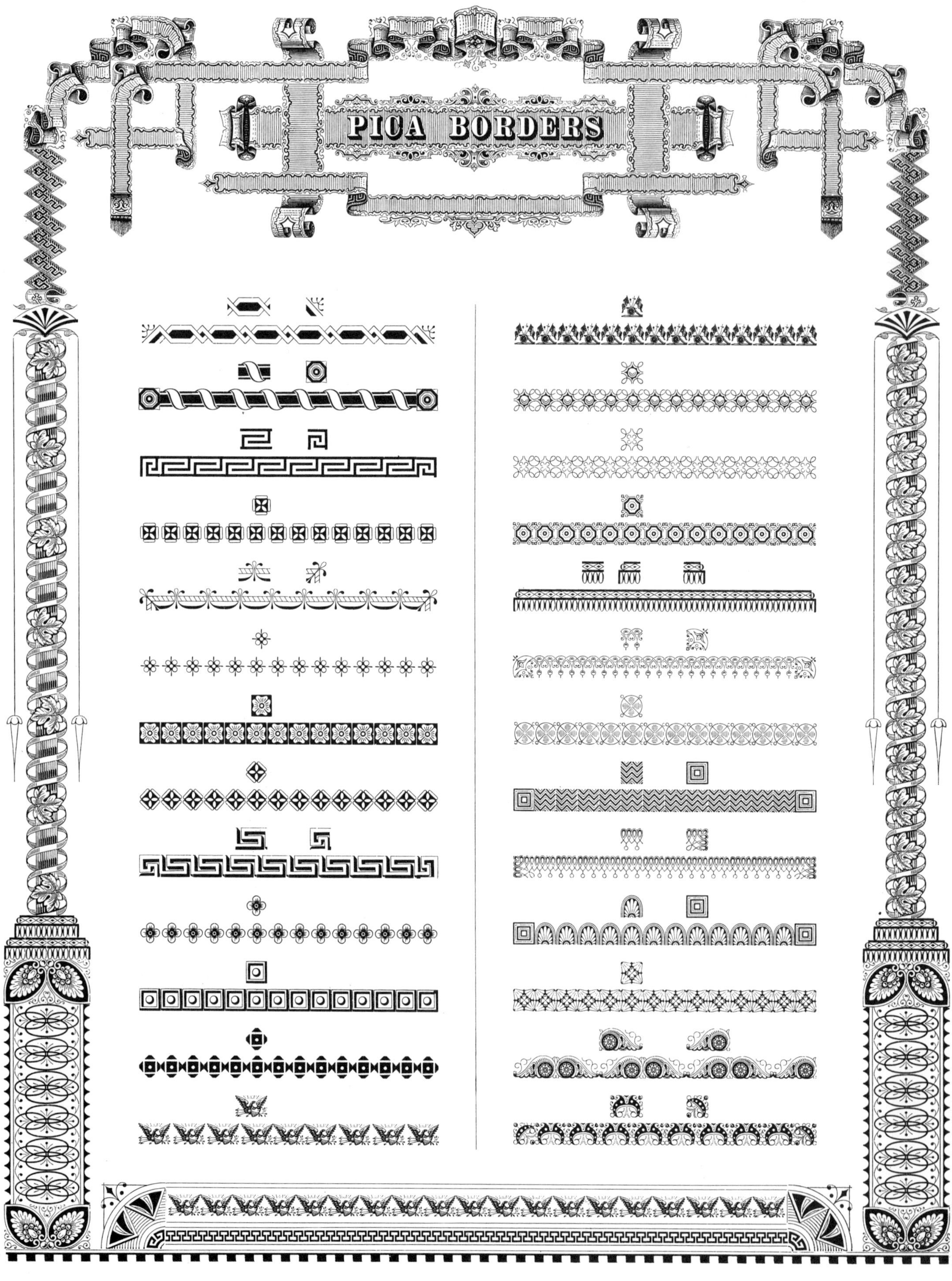
PICA BORDERS

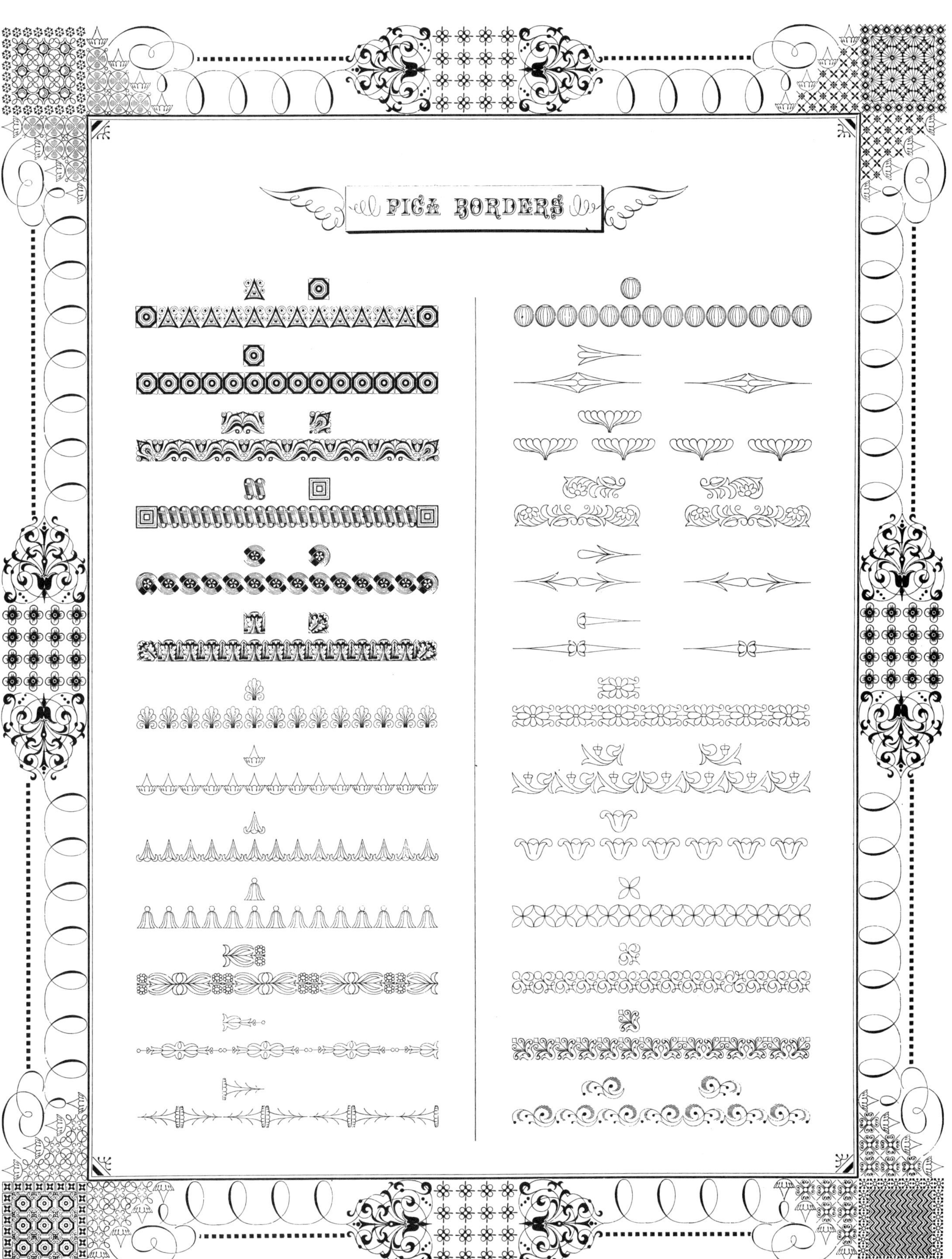
PICA BORDERS

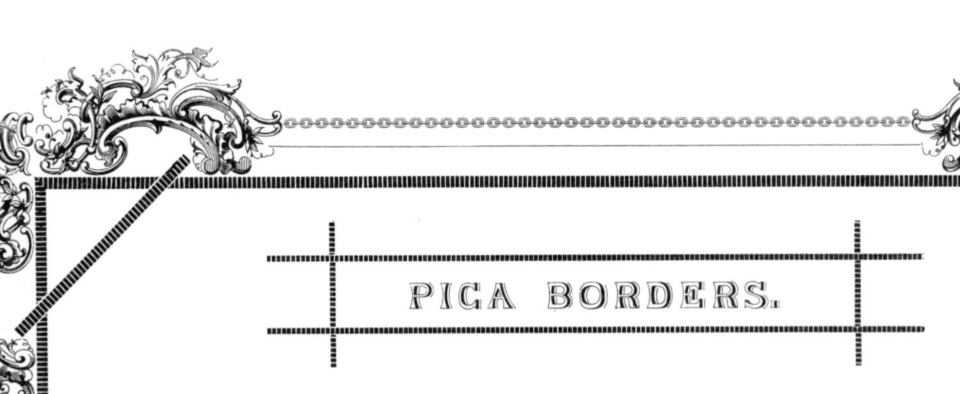

PICA BORDERS.

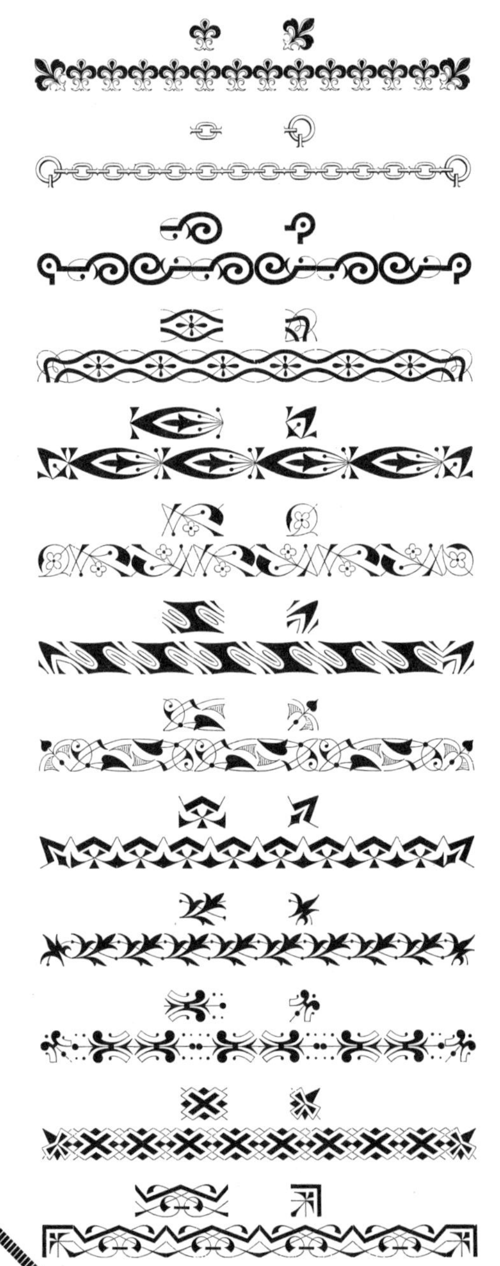

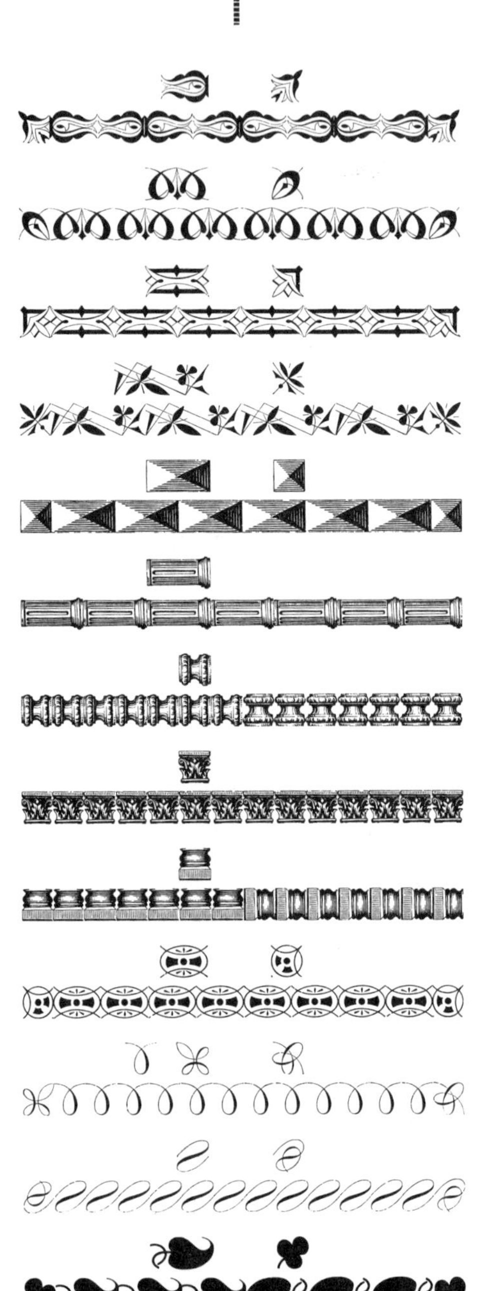

PICA BORDERS.

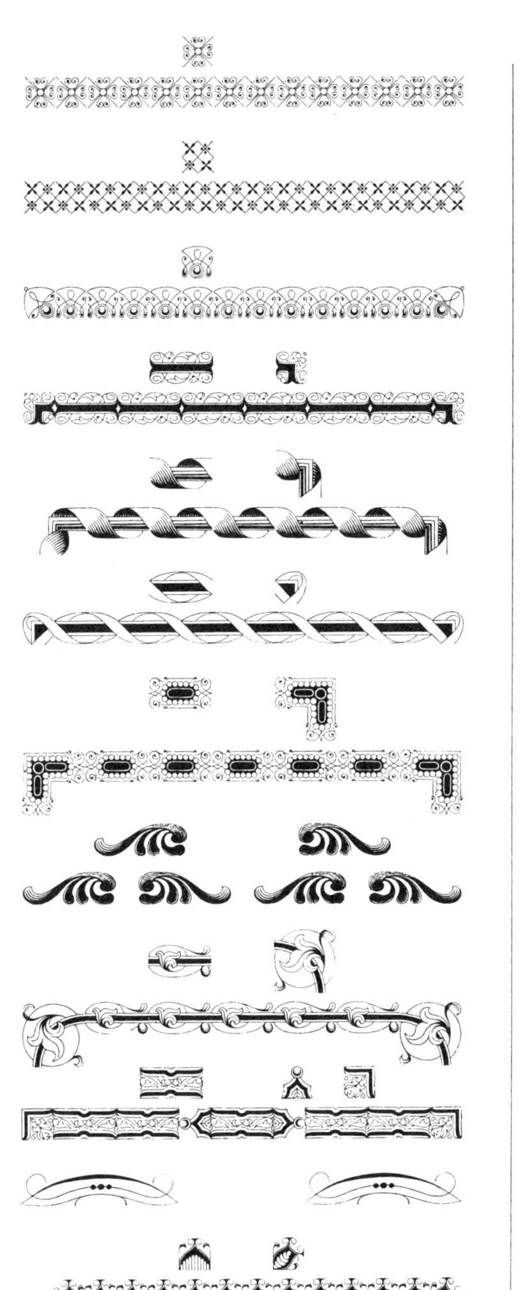

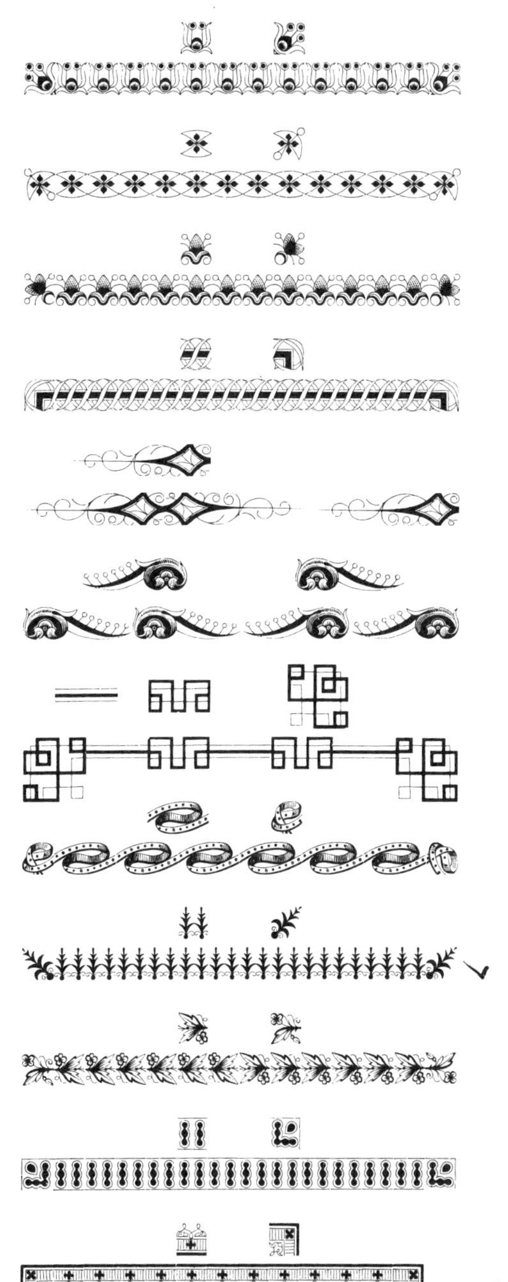

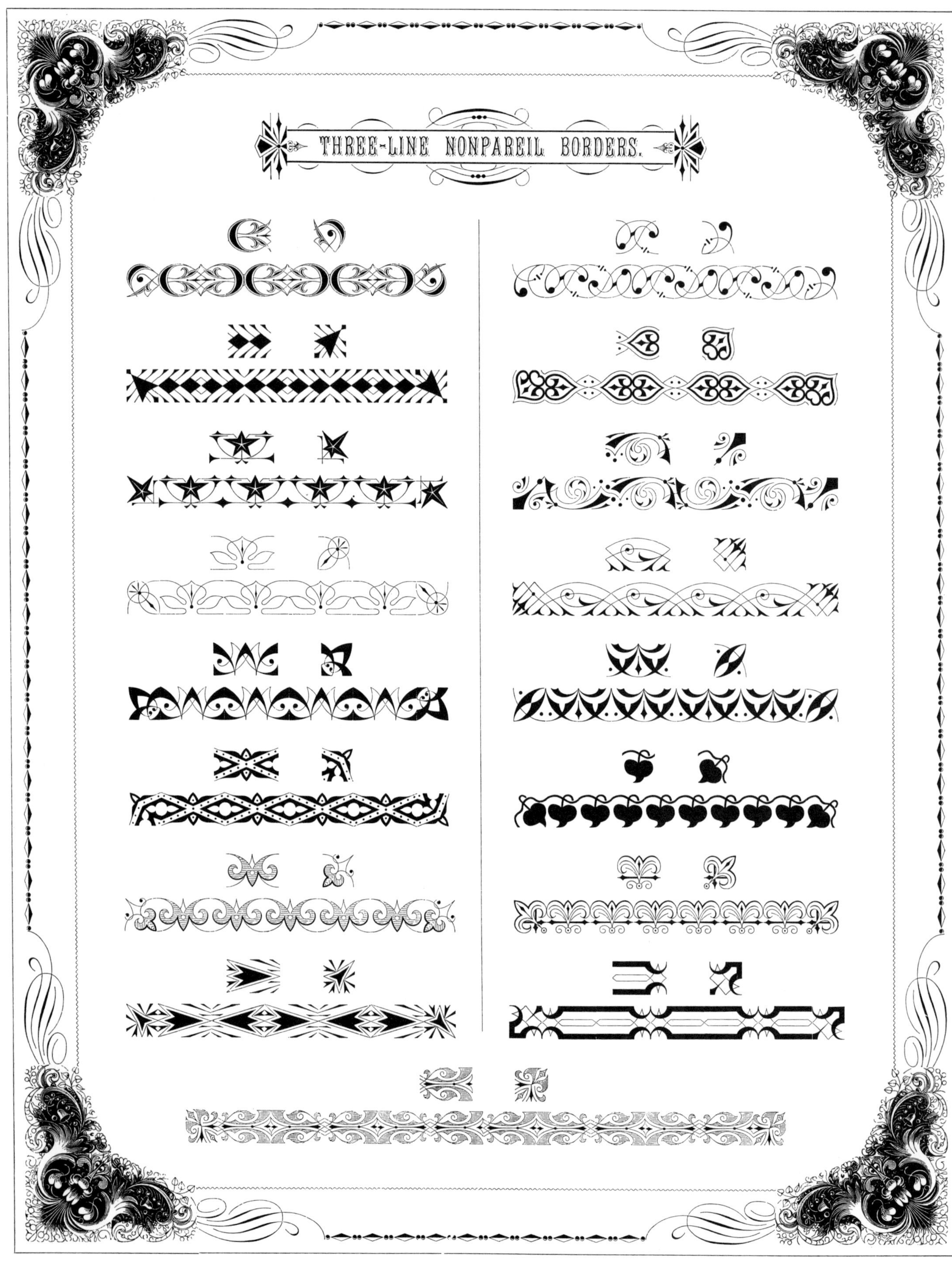
THREE-LINE NONPAREIL BORDERS.

THREE-LINE NONPAREIL BORDERS.

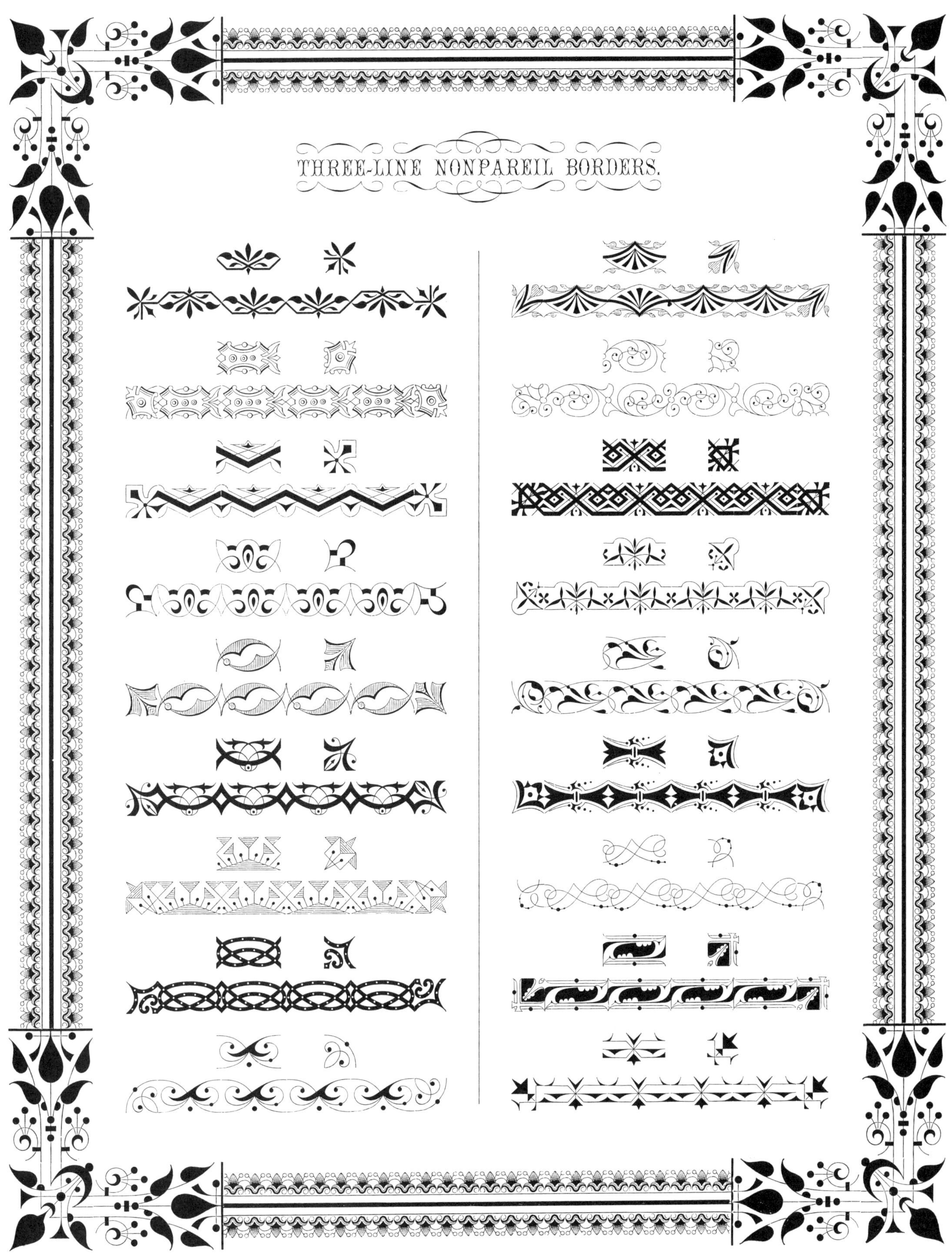

TWO-LINE PICA BORDERS.

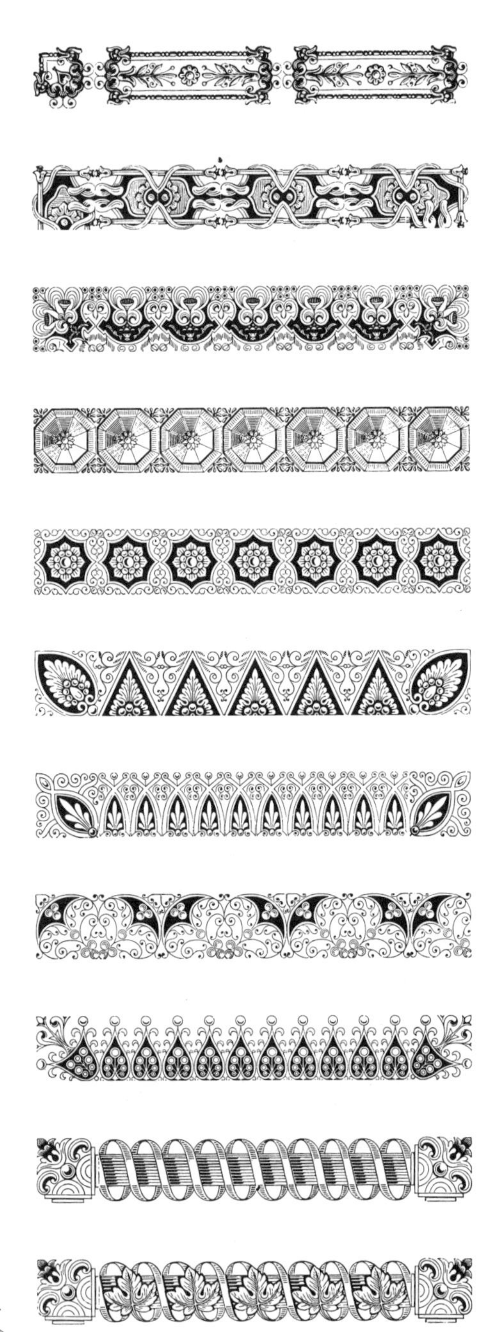

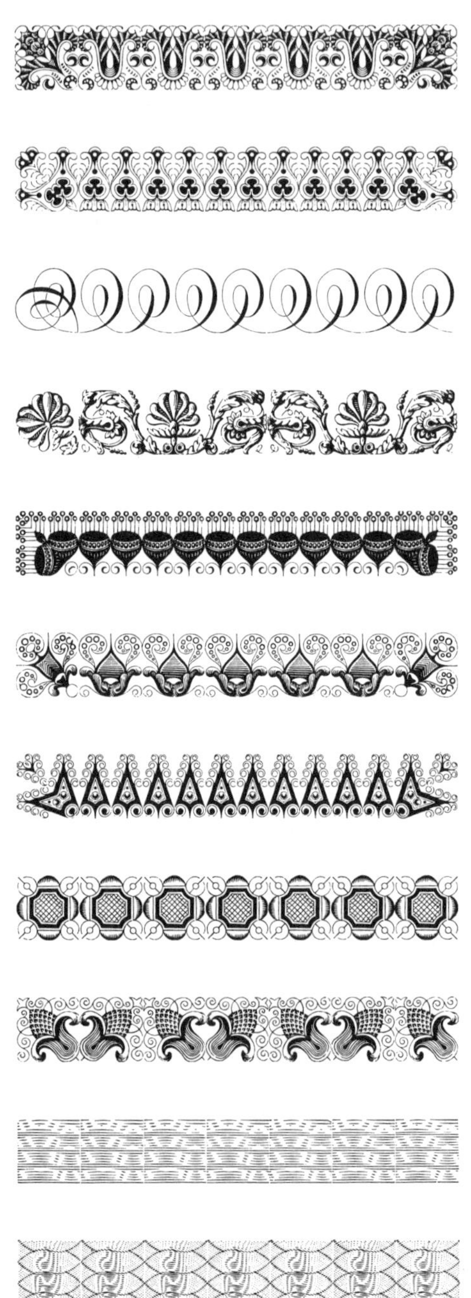

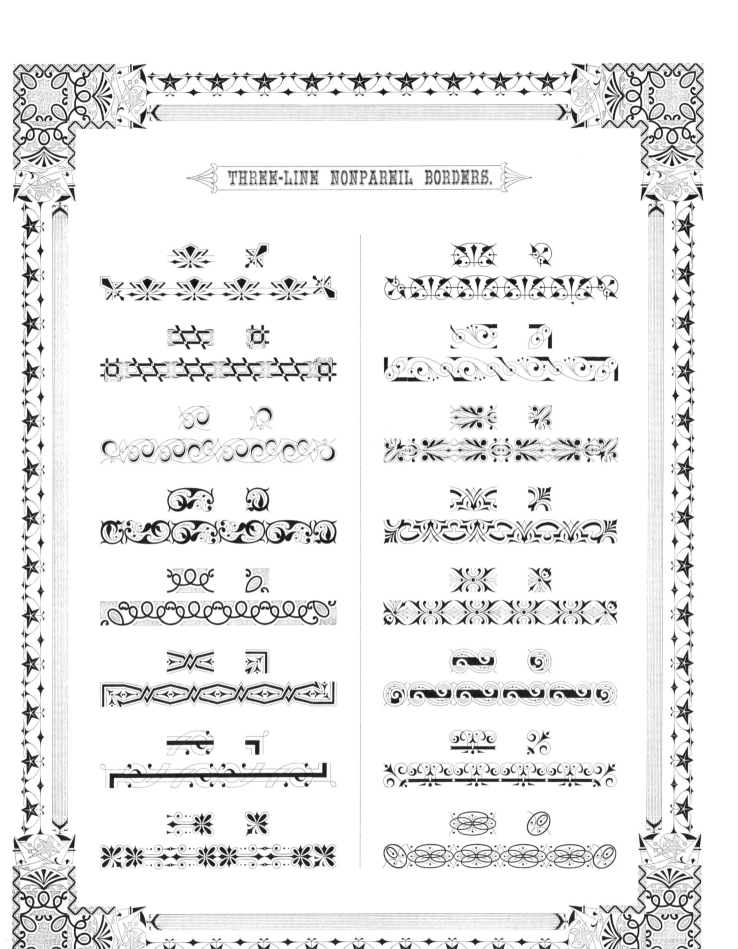

THREE-LINE NONPAREIL BORDERS.

TWO-LINE PICA BORDERS.

Two-line Pica Borders.

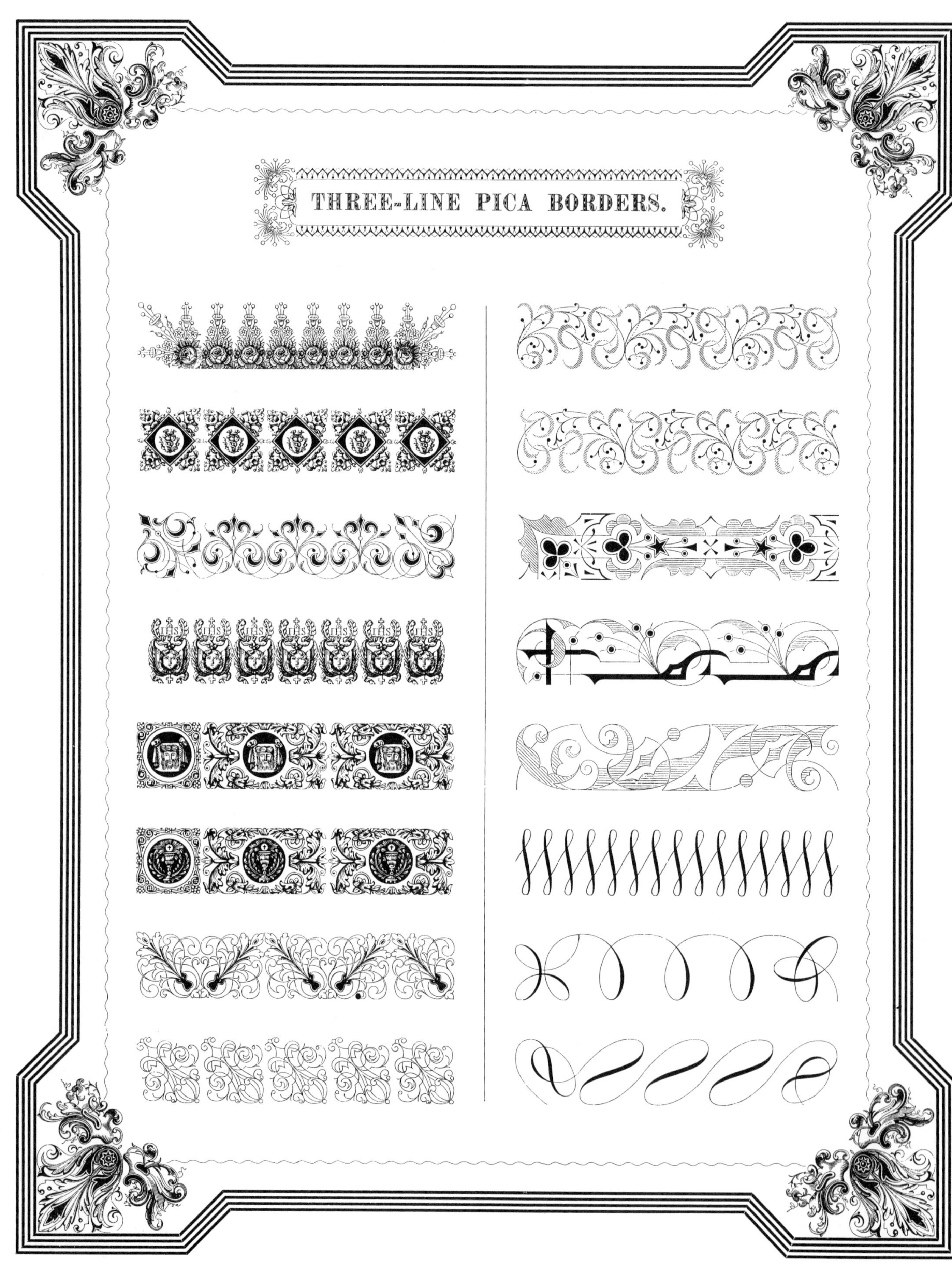
THREE-LINE PICA BORDERS.

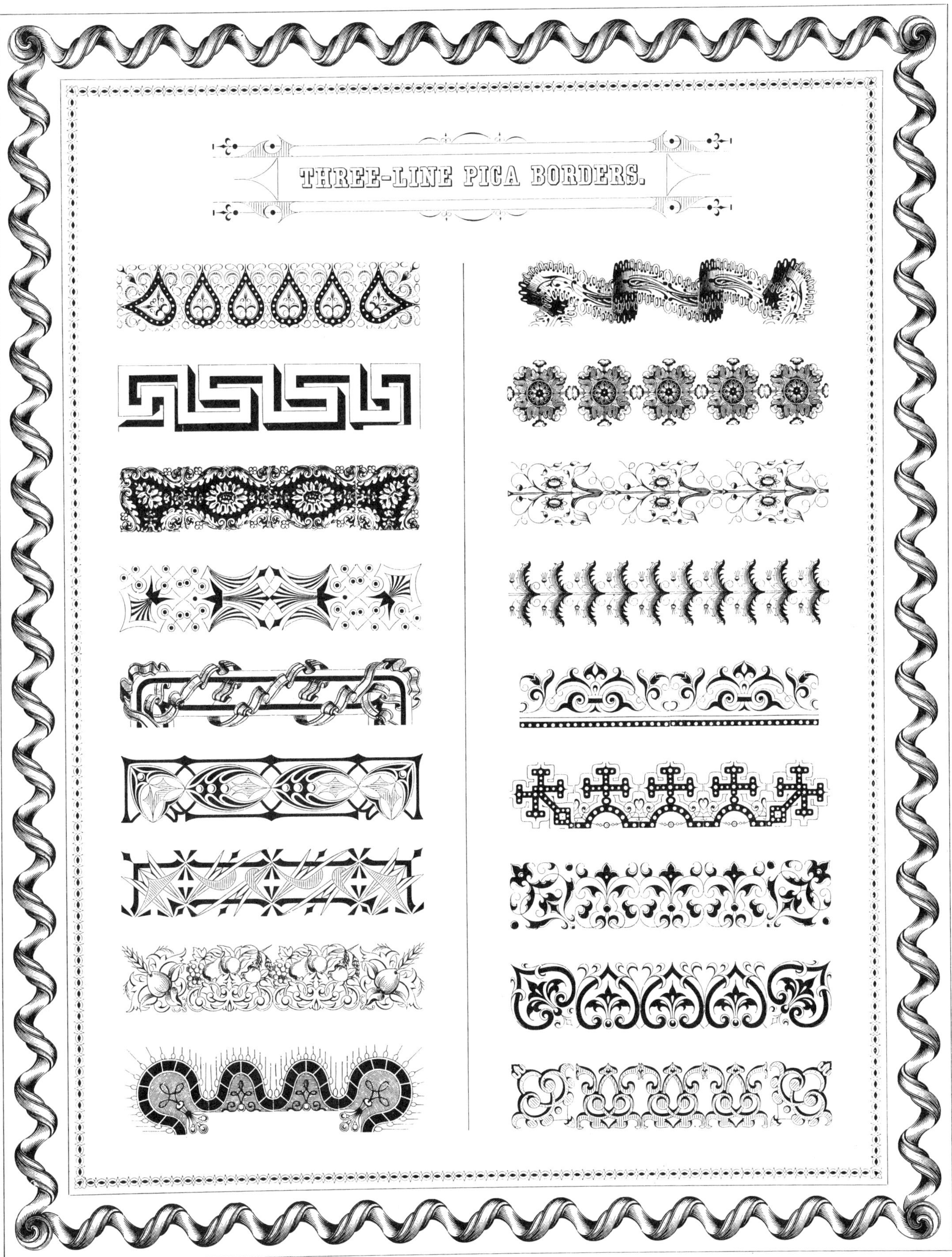
THREE-LINE PICA BORDERS.

FOUR-LINE PICA BORDERS.

Four-line Pica Borders.

FOUR-LINE PICA BORDERS.

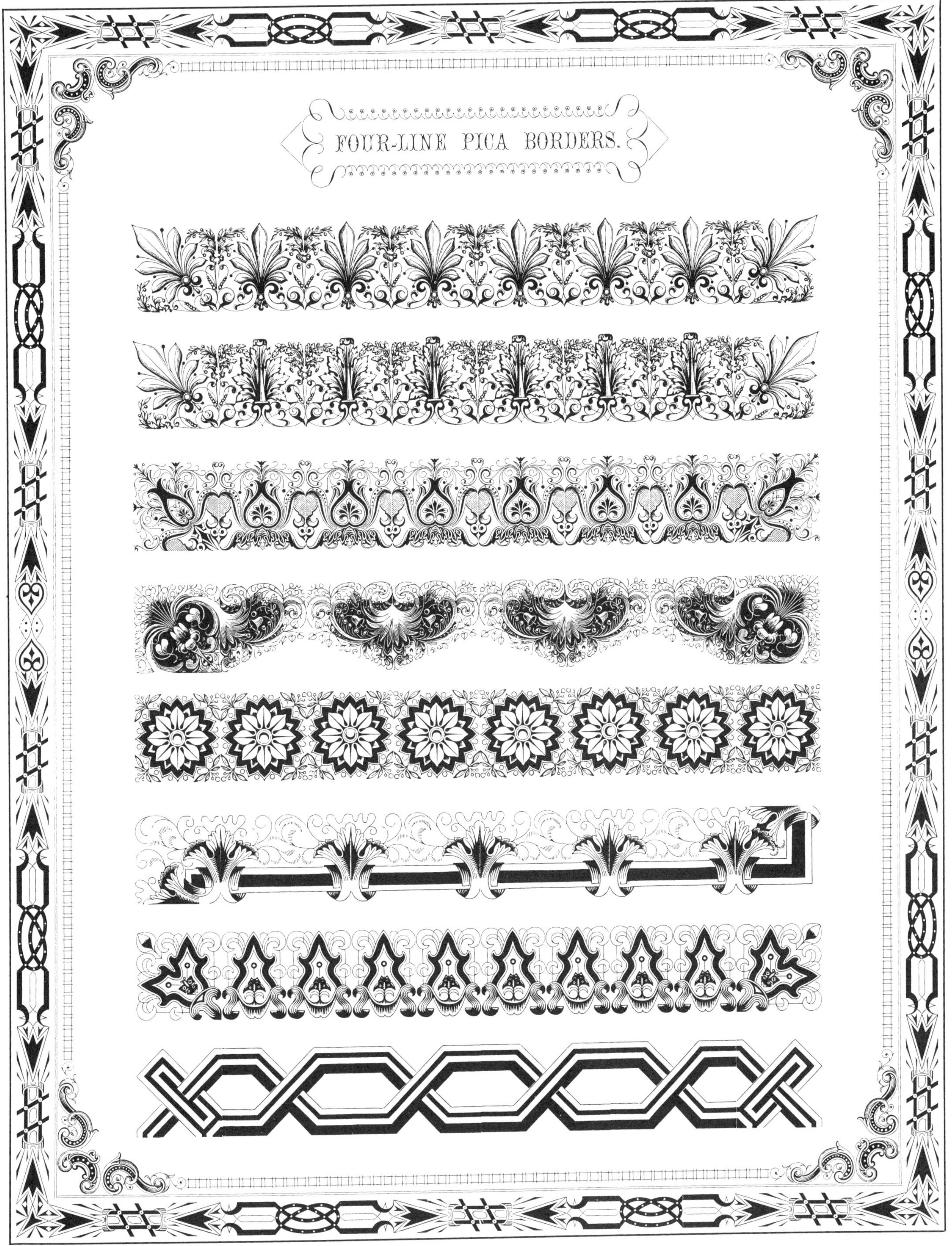
FOUR-LINE PICA BORDERS.

Five-line Pica Borders.

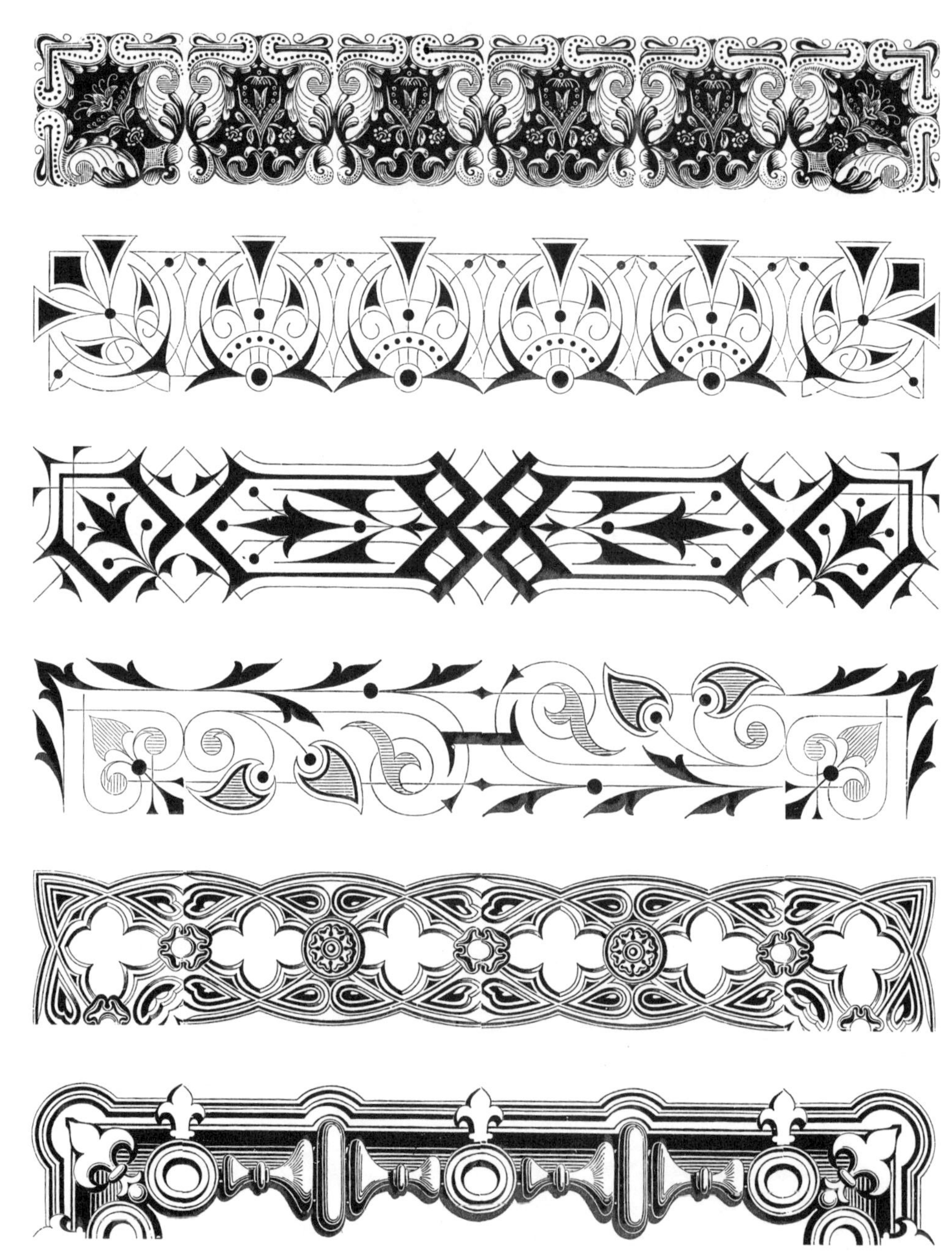

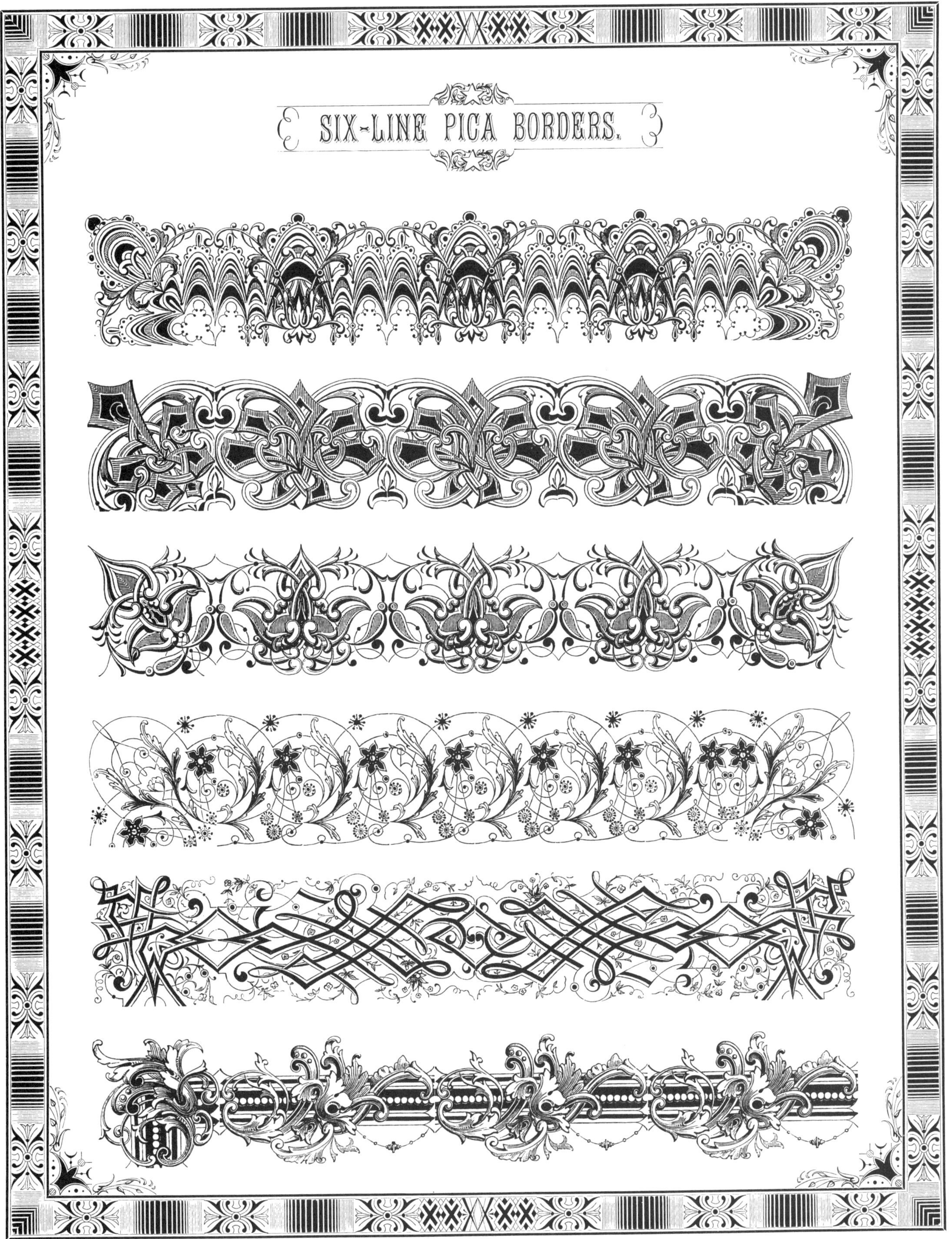
SIX-LINE PICA BORDERS.

Five-line Pica Borders.

SIX-LINE PICA BORDERS.
EIGHT-LINE PICA BORDERS.

18 BRUCE 81

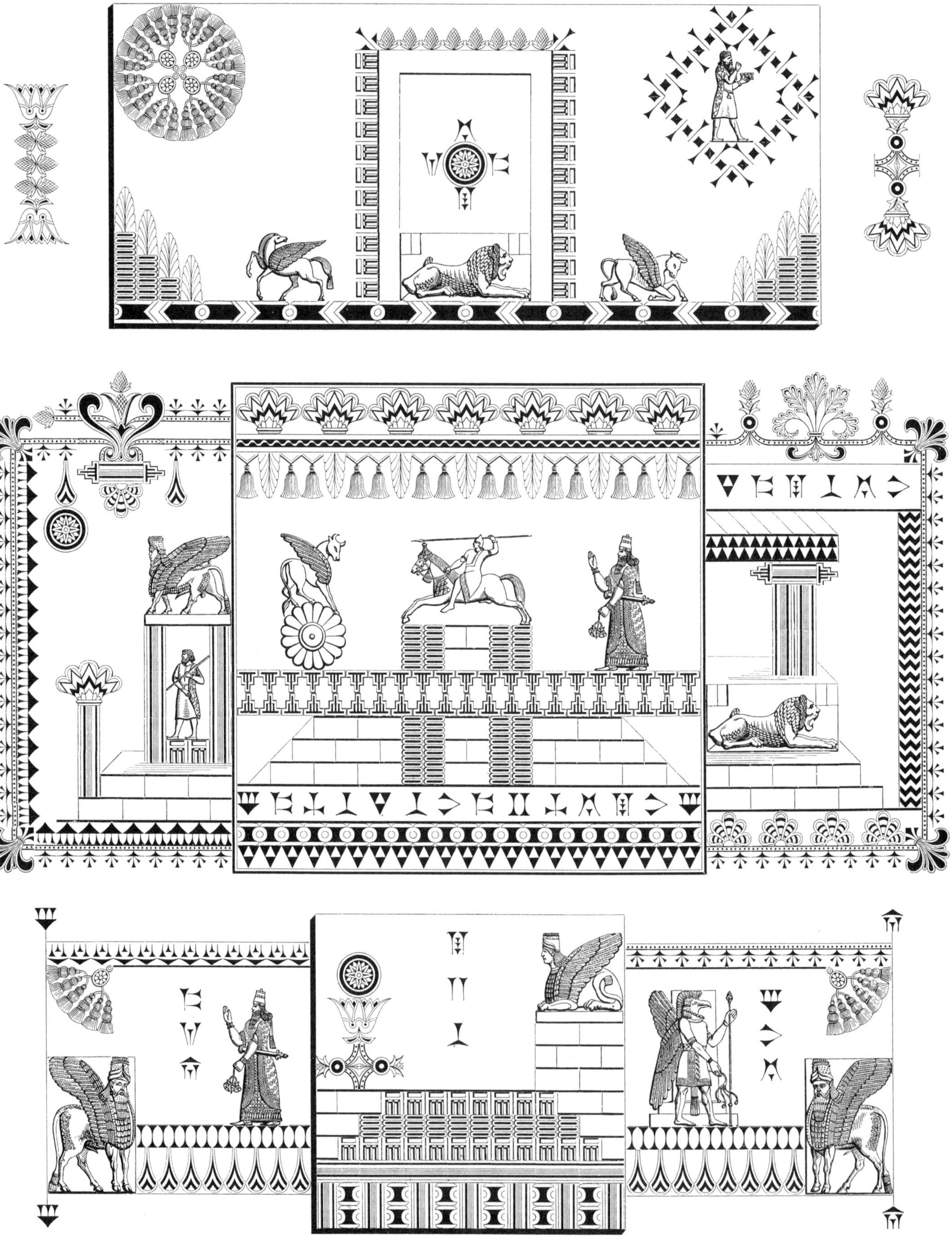

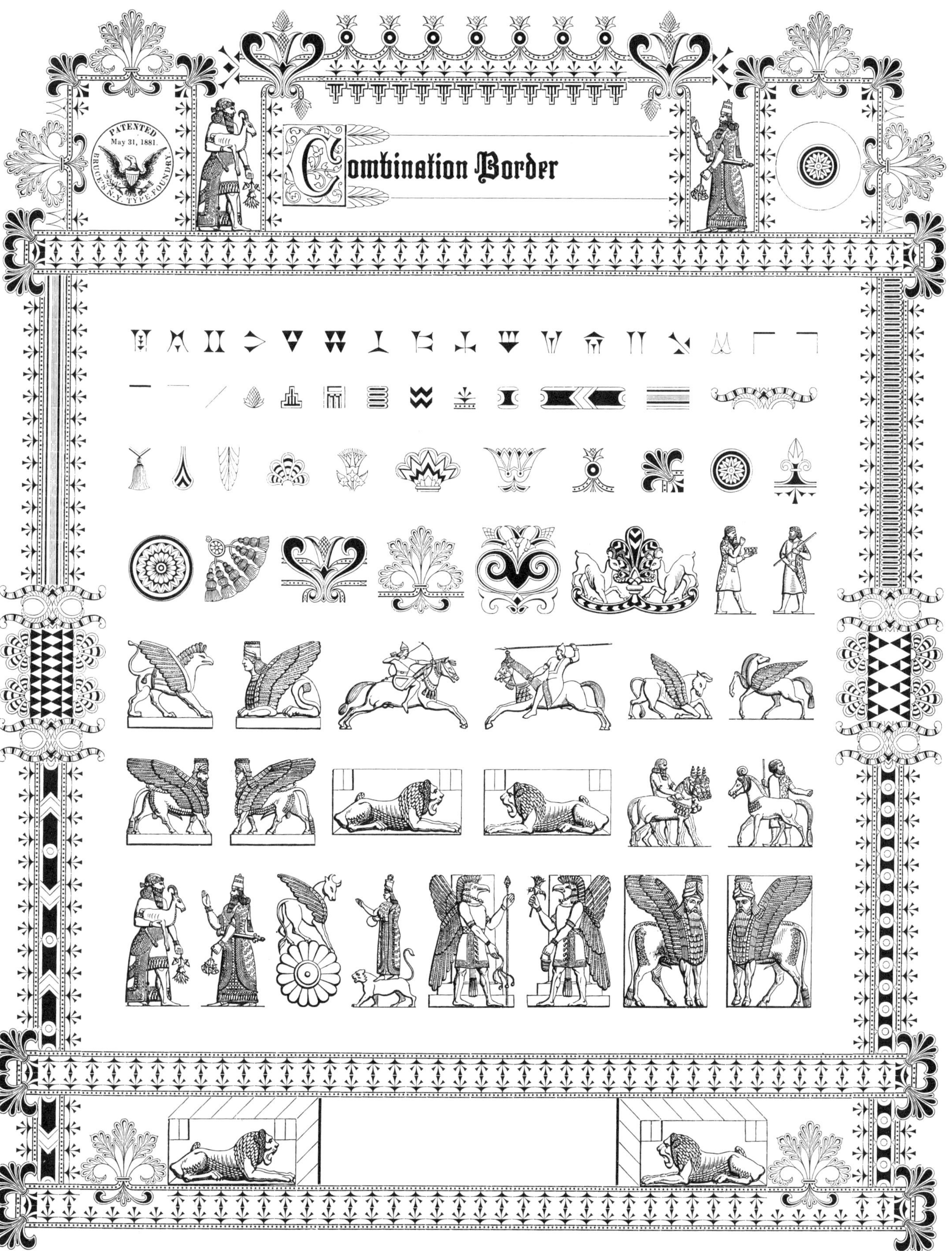
PATENTED
May 31, 1881.
BRUCE'S N.Y. TYPE FOUNDRY
Combination Border

COMBINATION BORDER

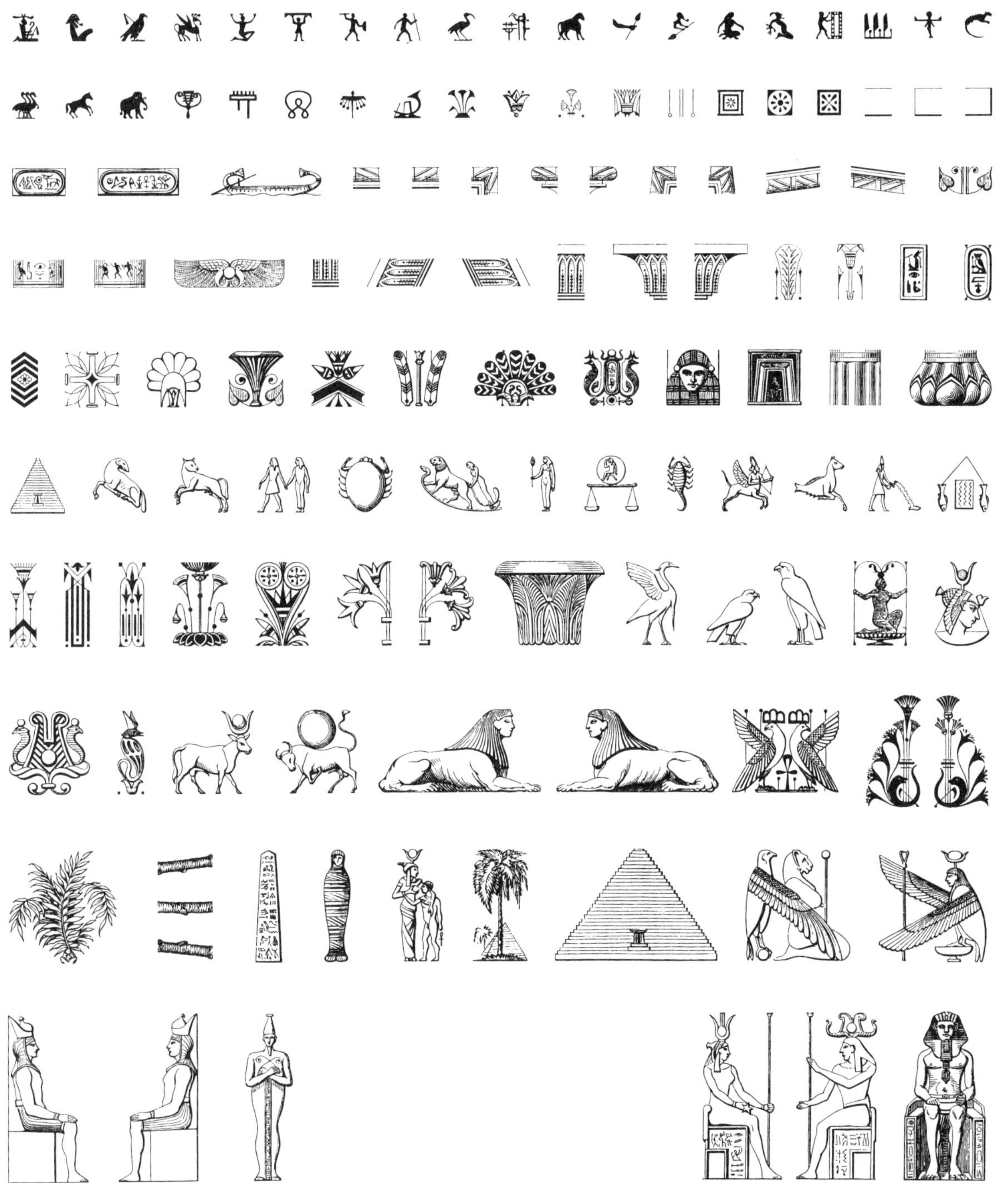

Corners for Brass Rule.

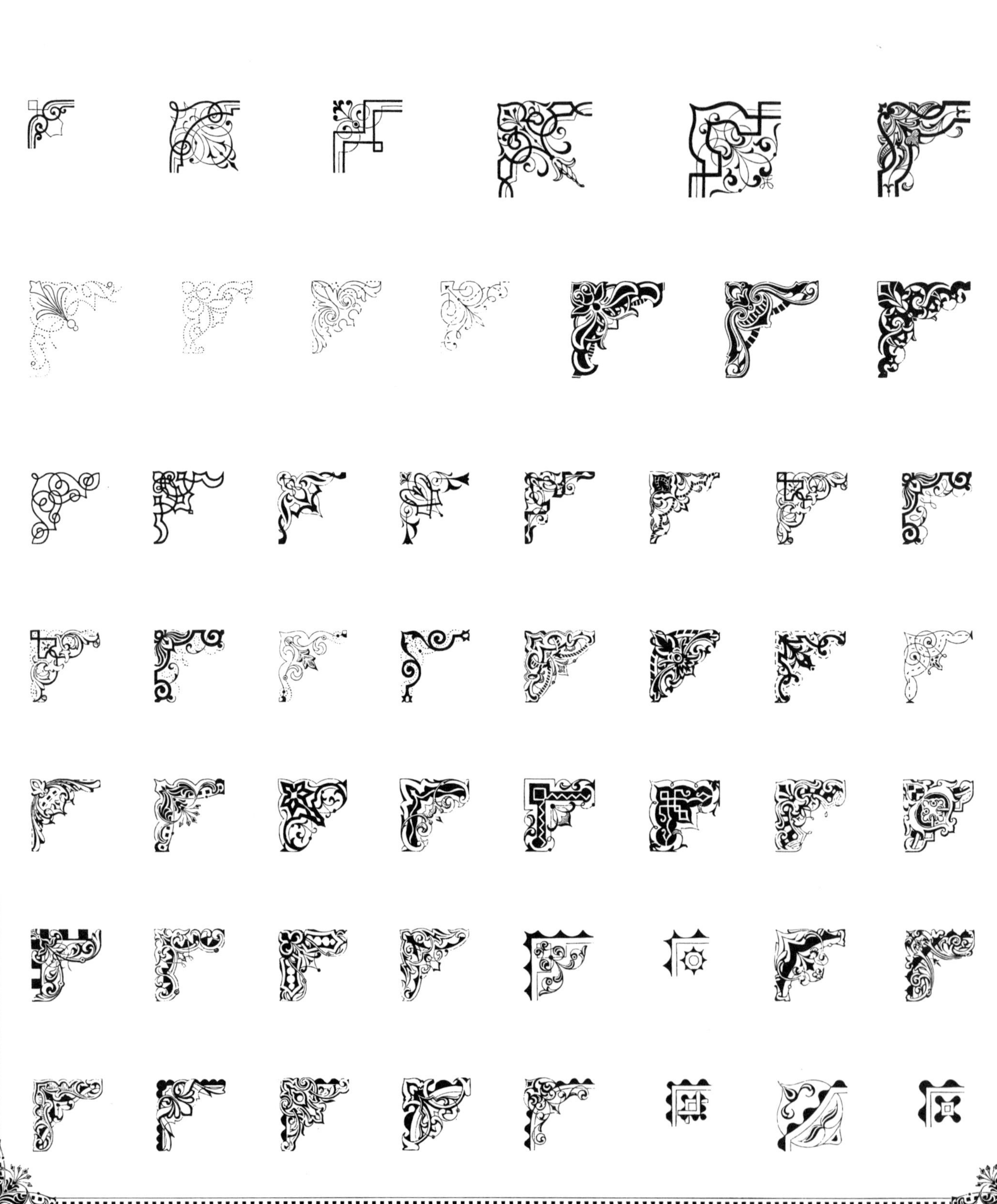

CORNERS FOR BRASS RULE.

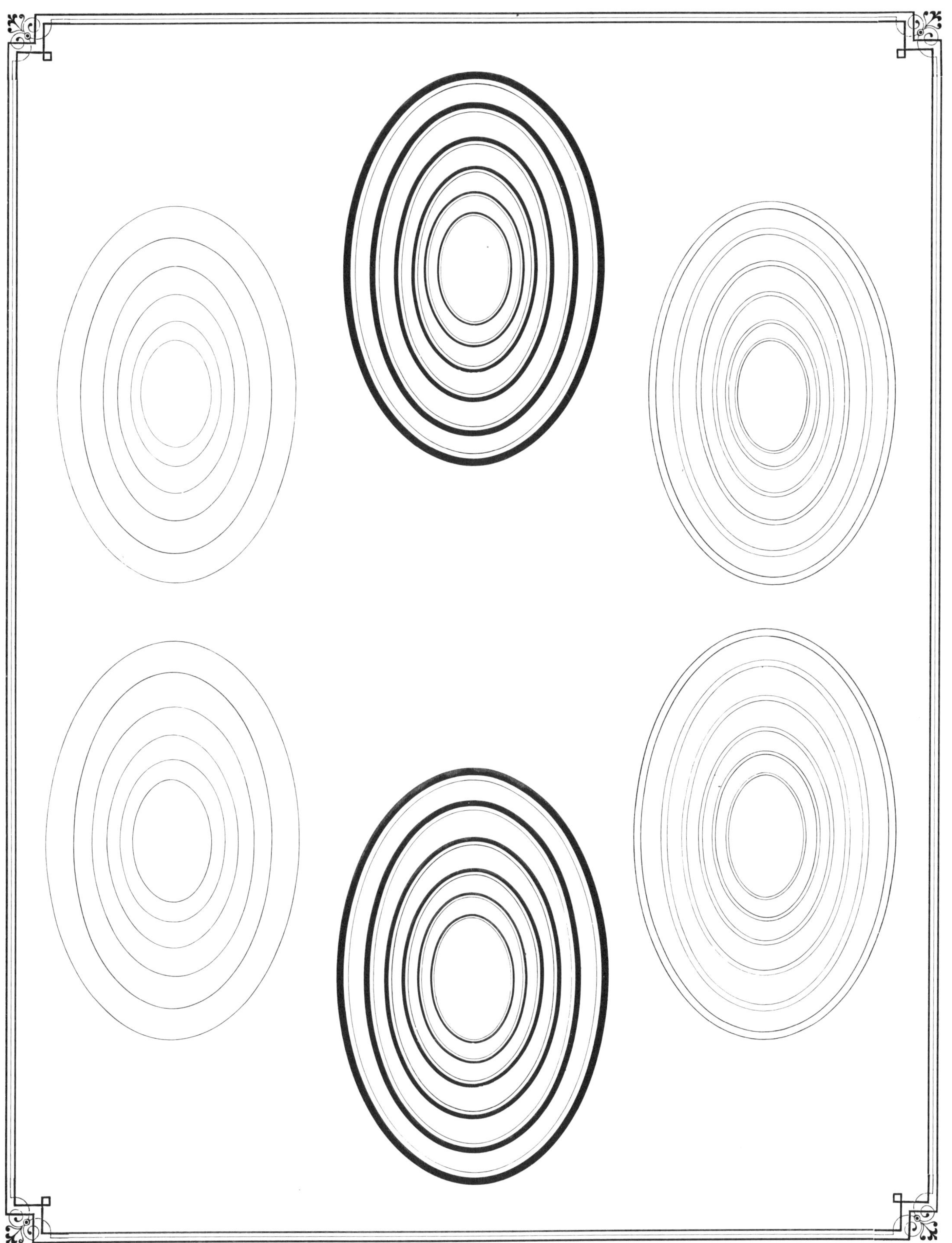

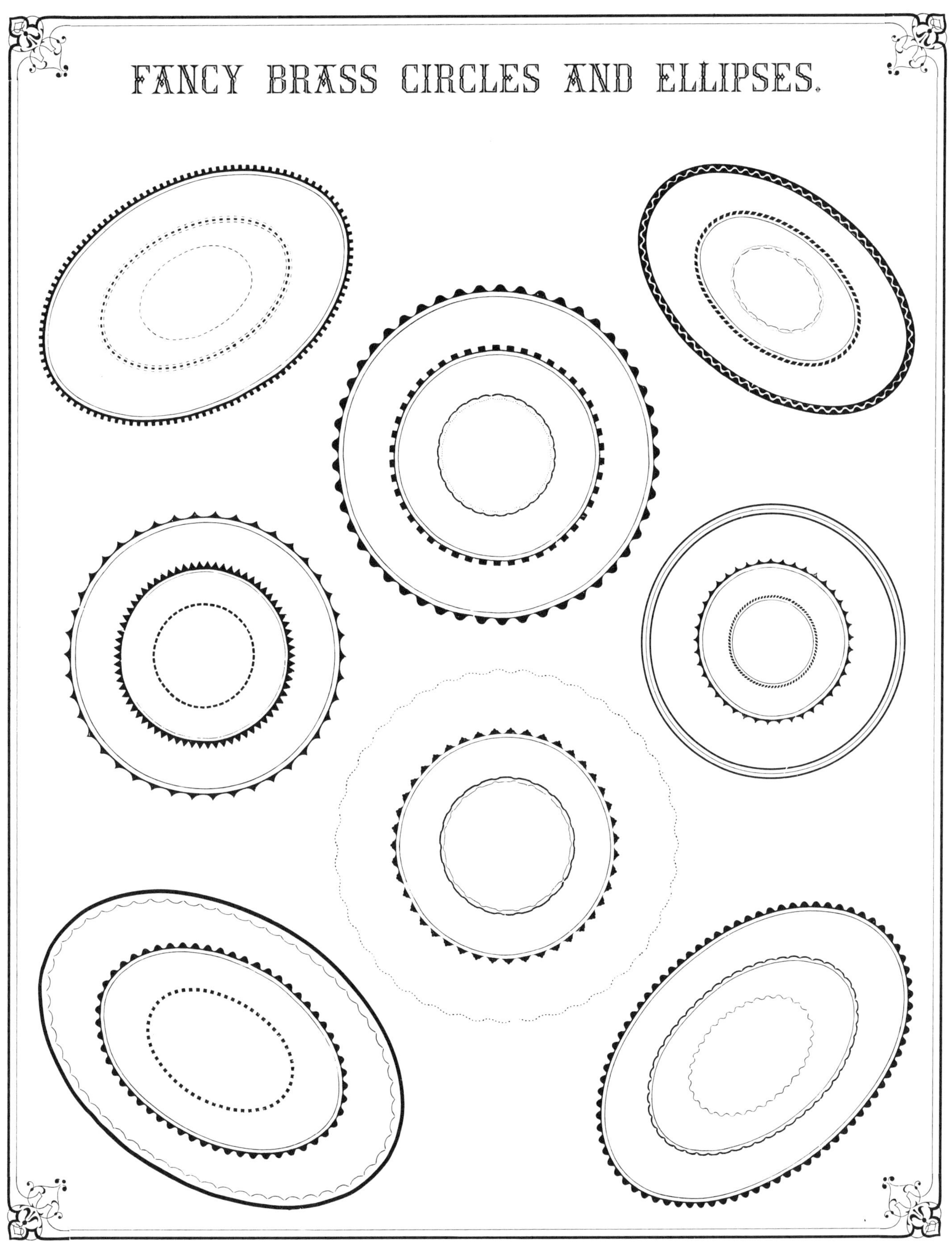
FANCY BRASS CIRCLES AND ELLIPSES.

Agriculture.

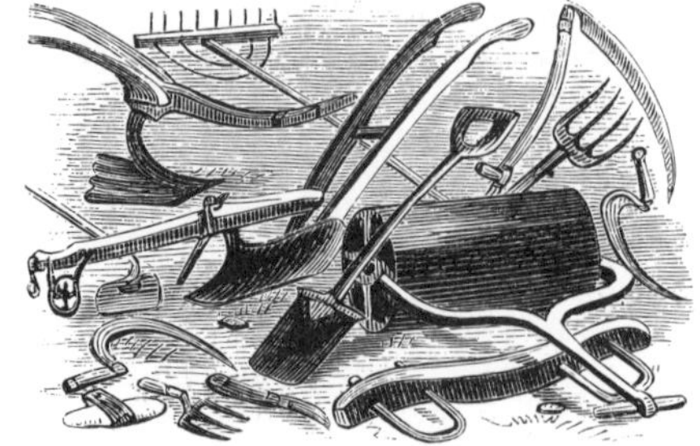
Agricultural Implements.

Apothecary.

Auctioneer.

Baker.

Billiards.

Boiler-maker.

Book-binder.

Bookstore.

Boot-maker. (Gent's)

Boot-maker. (Ladies')

Brewer.

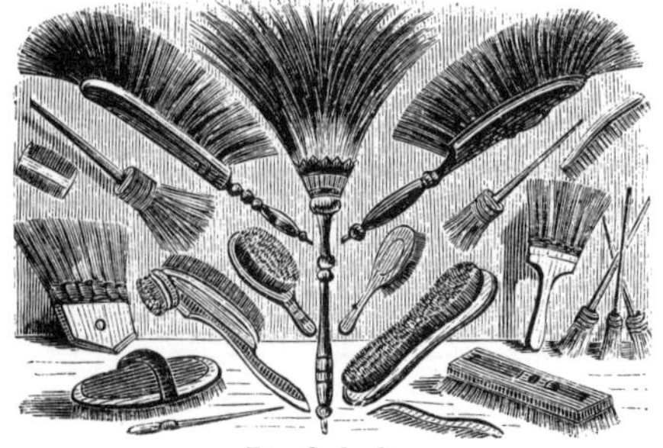
Brush-dealer.

Butcher.

Carpenter.

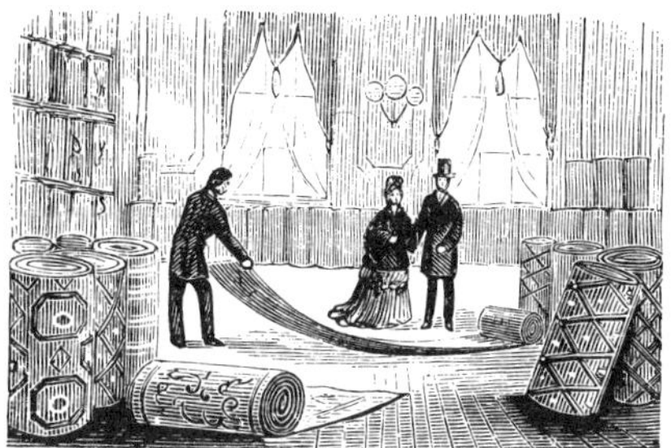
Carpets.

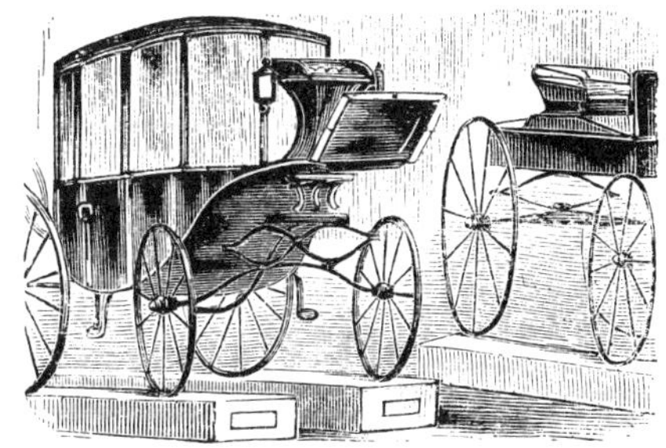
Carriages and Wagons.

Cattle-dealer.

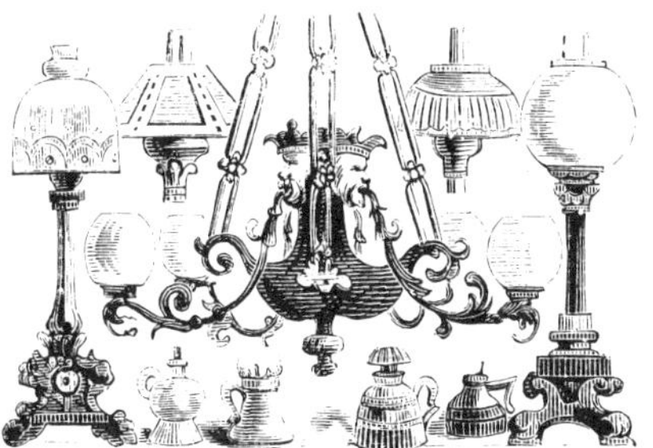
Chandeliers.

China and Glass-ware.

Coal-dealer.

Coal-miner.

Confectionery.

Cooper.

Cutler.

Dentist.

Dress-maker.

Driving.

Dry Goods.

Express.

Farmer.

Fish-dealer.

Fishing-Tackle.

Florist.

Flour and Feed.

Fruit.

Furniture.

Furrier.

Gas-fixtures.

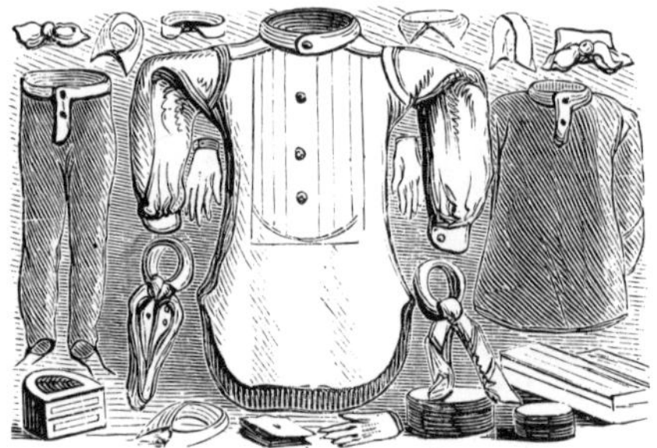
Gentlemen's Furnishing.

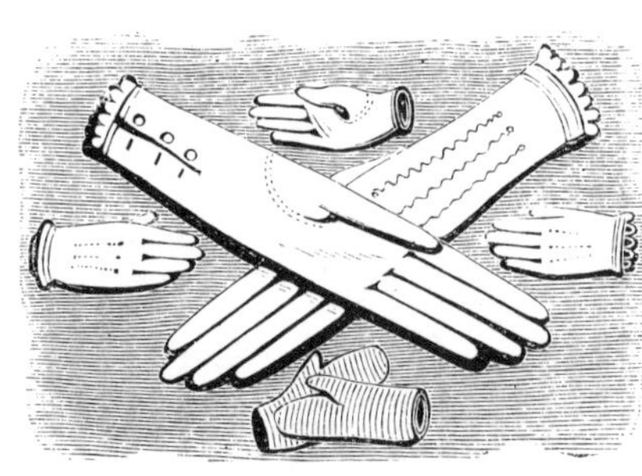
Glover.

Grocer.

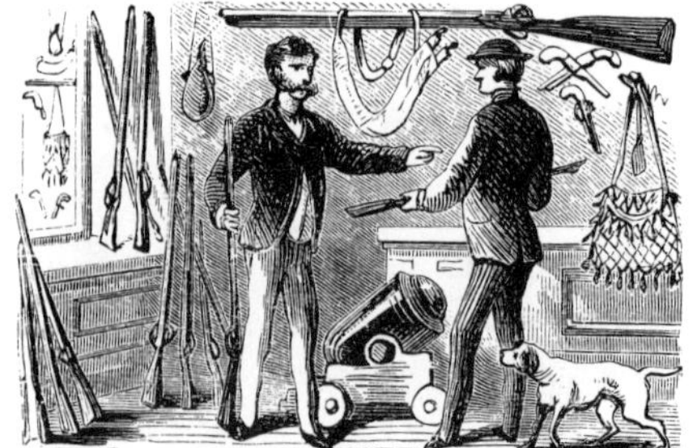
Gunsmith.

Hair--dresser. (Gent's)

Hair-dresser. (Ladies')

Hardware.

Hatter.

Horse-dealer.

Horseshoer.

Hosiery.

Ice.

Jeweler.

Kitchen-furnishings.

Lager-beer.

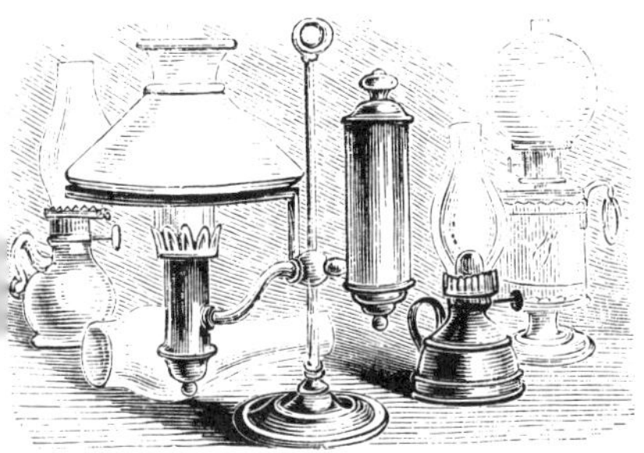
Lamp-dealer.

Livery-stable

Lock-smith and Bell-hanger.

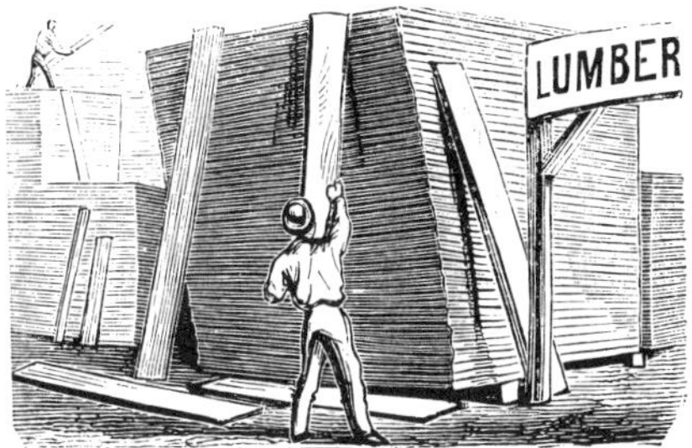

Lumber-dealer.

Machinist.

Marble-works.

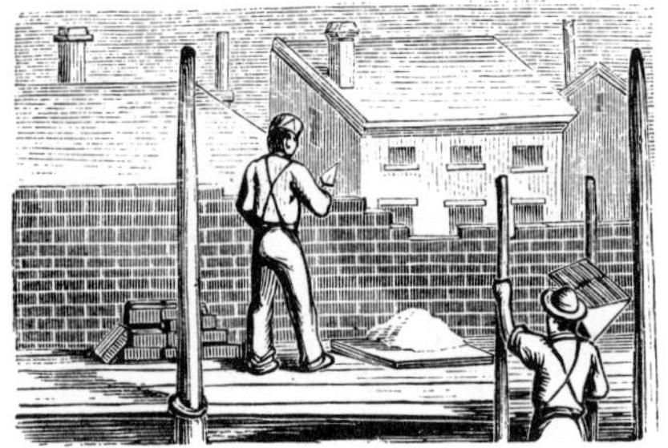
Mason.

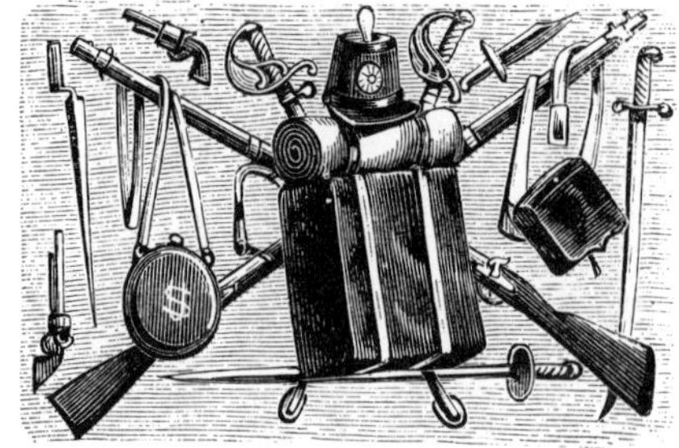
Military Goods.

Millinery.

Mineral Water.

Musical Instruments.

Music. (Instrumental)

Music. (Military)

Music. (Piano)

Music. (Sacred)

Music. (Vocal)

Naval.

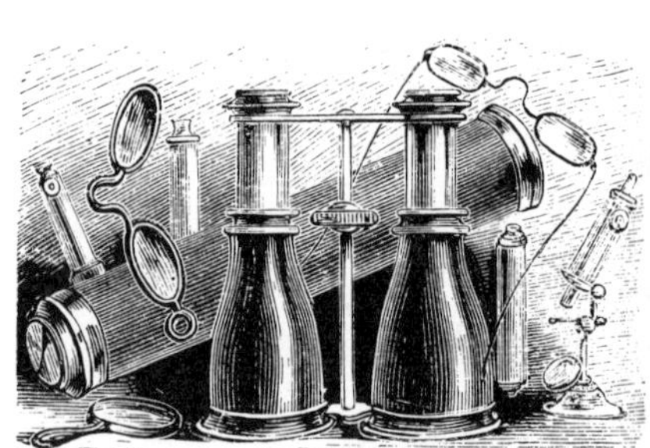
Optician.

Oyster-house.

Painter. (House)

Painter. (Sign)

Paper-hanger.

Piano-dealer.

Pickles.

Picture-frames.

Photographer.

Planter. (Cotton)

Planter. (Sugar)

Planter. (Tobacco)

Plumber.

Printer. (Compositor)

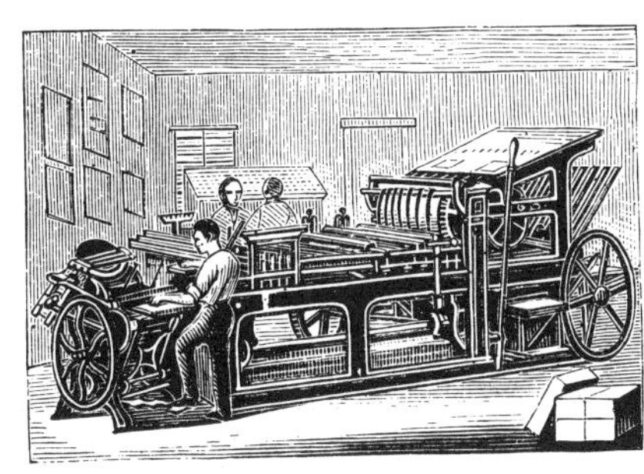
Printer. (Press)

Race. (Boat)

Race. (Horse)

Race. (Yacht)

Railroad. (Freight)

Restaurant.

Saddlery.

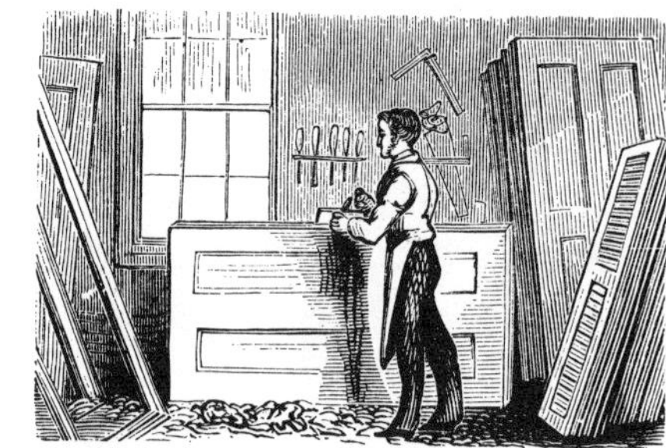
Sashes, Blinds and Doors.

Schooner.

Segar-dealer.

Sewing-Machine.

Ship-builder.

Shipping.

Shipping.

Silverware.

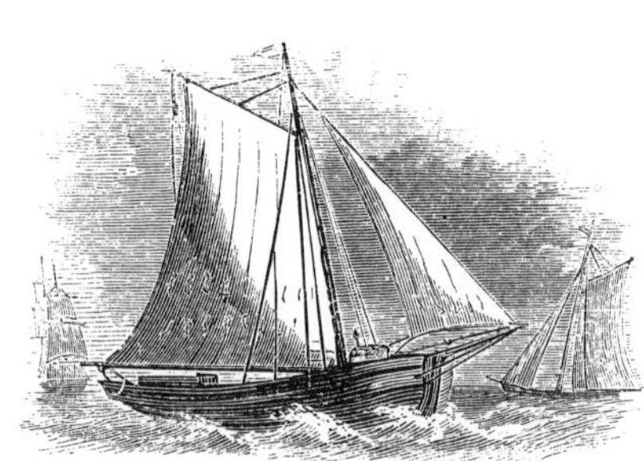
Sloop.

Stationer.

Steam-boat.

Steam-engine.

Steam Fire-engine.

Steam-ship.

Steam-ship.

Stoves.

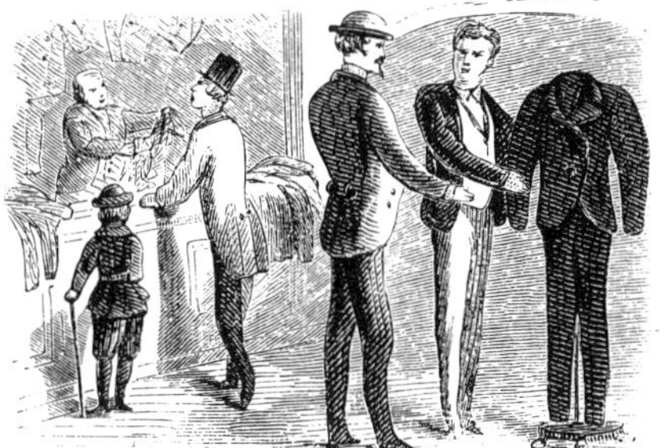
Tailor.

Tanner.

Tea-dealer.

Theatrical.

Tin-ware.

Tobacco-pipe Dealer.

Toy-dealer.

Trunks.

Tug-boat.

Umbrella-dealer.

Undertaker.

Upholsterer.

Wagon-riding.

Watches and Clocks.

Wheelwright.

Wine and Beer Garden.

Wine-dealer.

Willow-ware.

Wooden-ware.

Yankee Notions.

Agriculture.

Agricultural Implts.

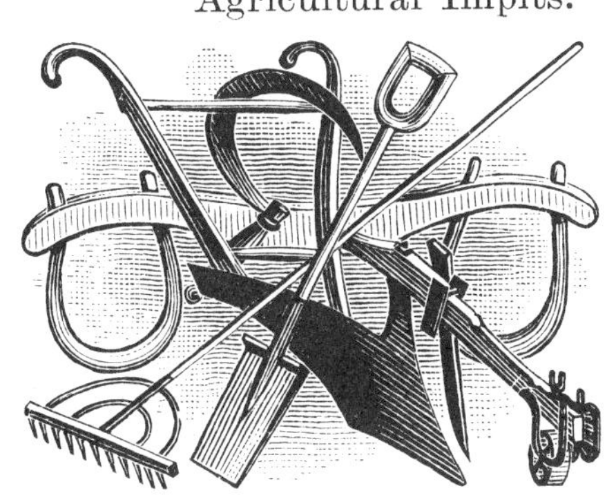

Apothecary.

Artificial Flowers.

Auctioneer.

Baker.

Book-binder.

Bookstore.

Boot-maker. (Gent's)

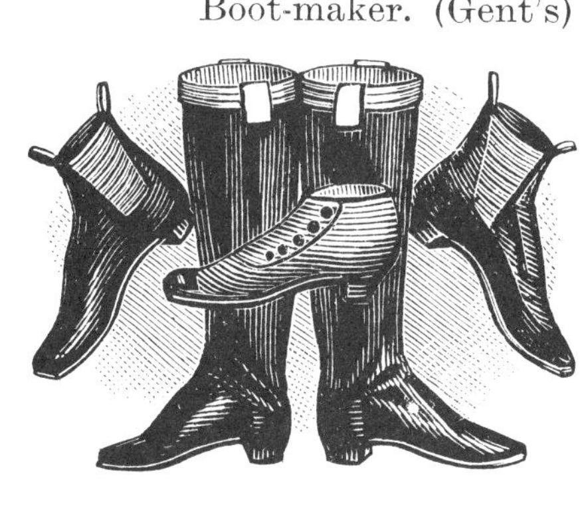

Billiards.

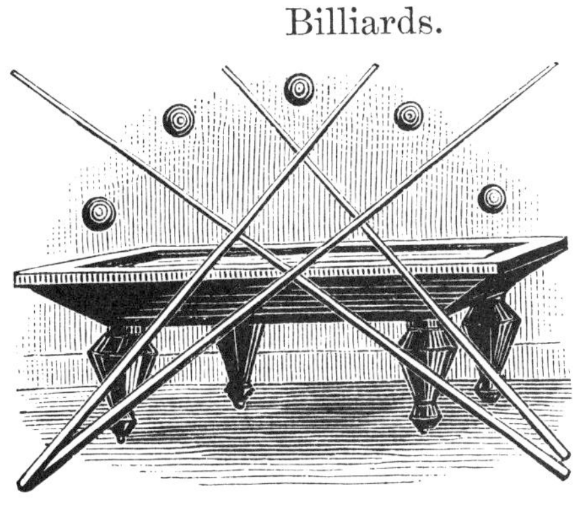

Blacksmith.

Blinds and Shades.

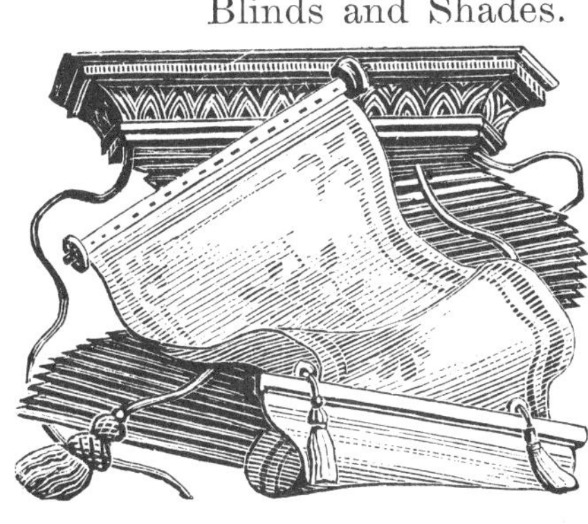

Boiler-maker.

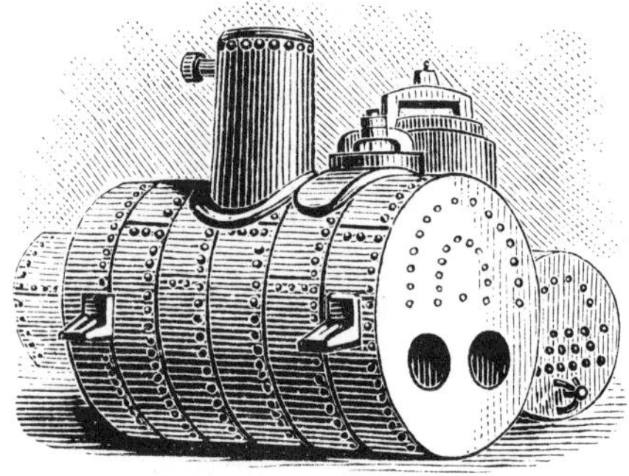

Boot-maker. (Ladies')

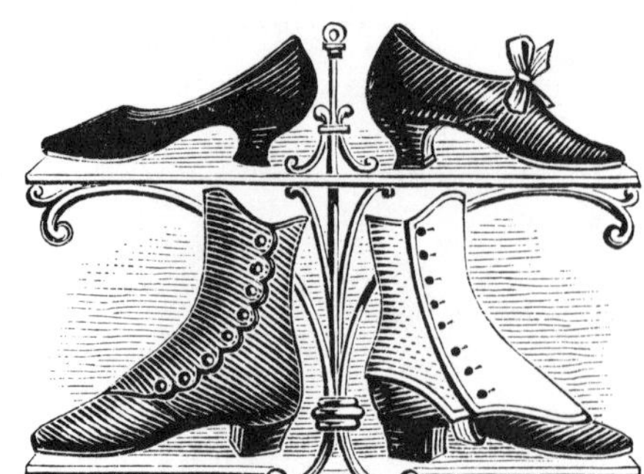

Brass-founder.

Brewer.

Bric-a-brac.

Brush-dealer.

Butcher.

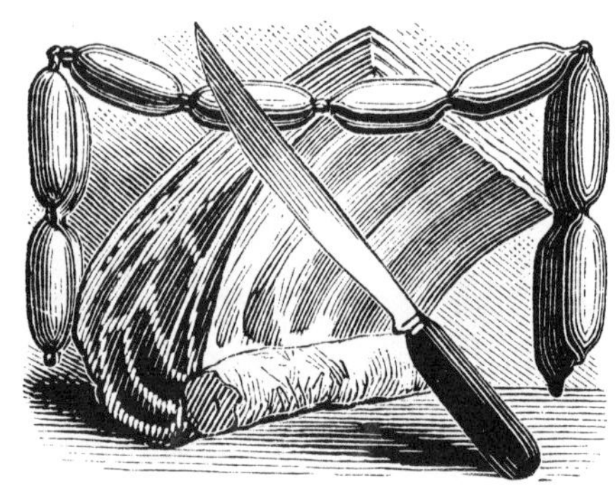

Carpenter.

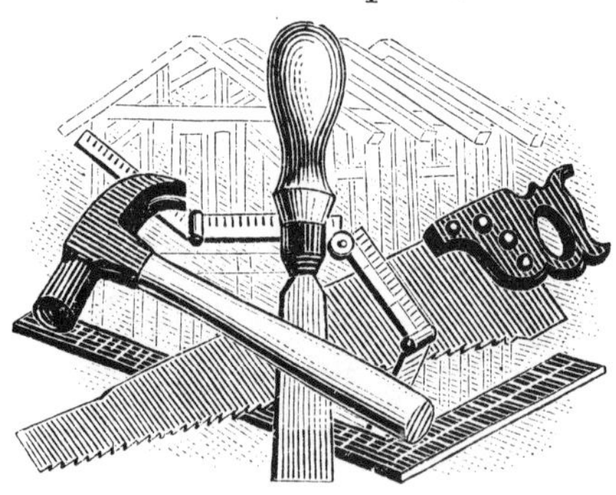

Carpets.

Carriages & Wagons.

Cattle-dealer.

Chair-maker.

Chandeliers & Lamps.

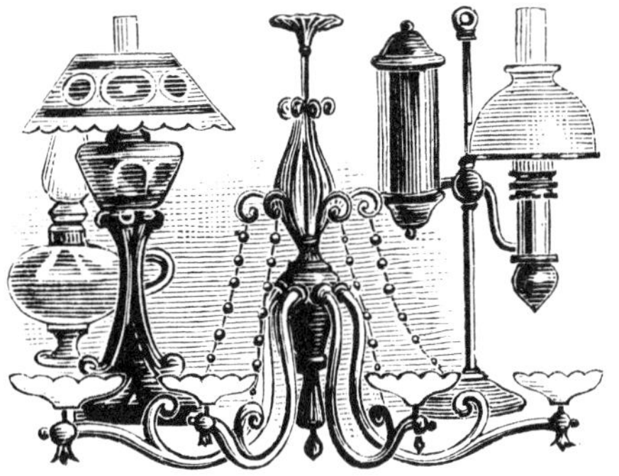

China & Glass-ware.

Coal-dealer.

Comb-dealer.

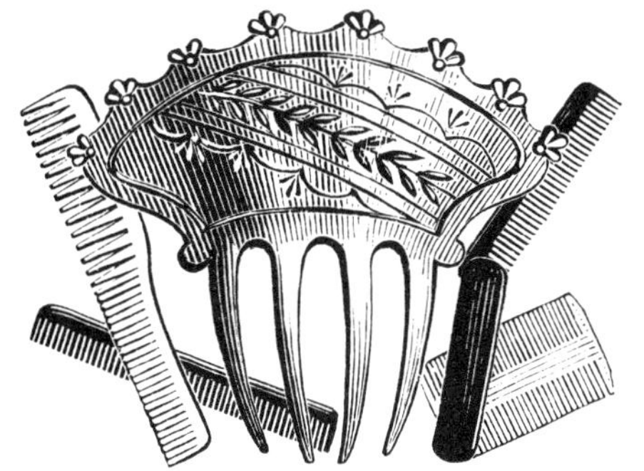

Confectioner.

Cooper.

Copper-smith.

Cutler.

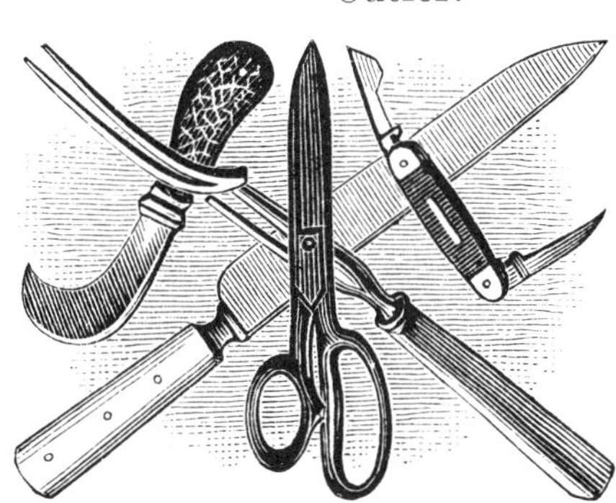

Dairy.

Dentist.

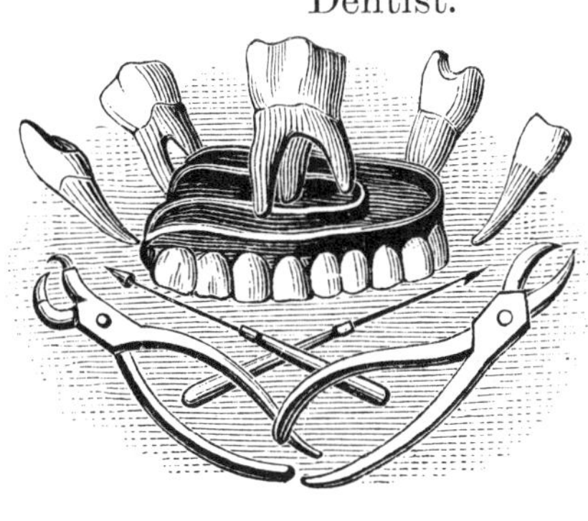

Dog-dealer.

Dress-maker.

Kitchen-furnishing.

Lager-Beer.

Lamps and Oil.

Leather-dealer.

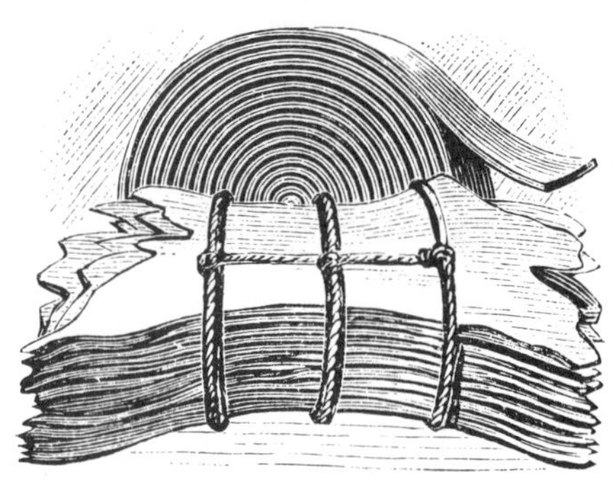

Liquor-dealer.

Livery-Stable.

Lock-s'th & Bell-hanger.

Locomotive.

Lumber-dealer.

Machinist.

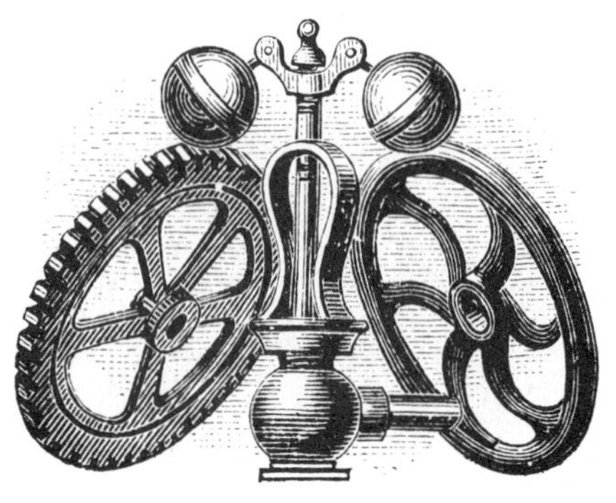

Marble-cutter.

Mason.

Masonic.

Milinery.

Military Goods.

Mineral Waters.

Musical Instruments.

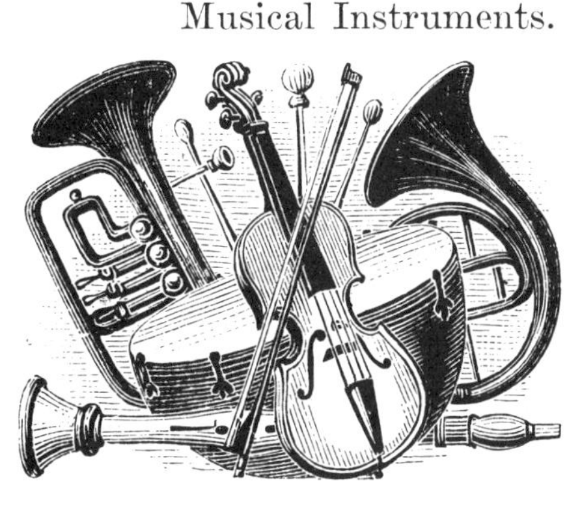

Music-store.

Naval.

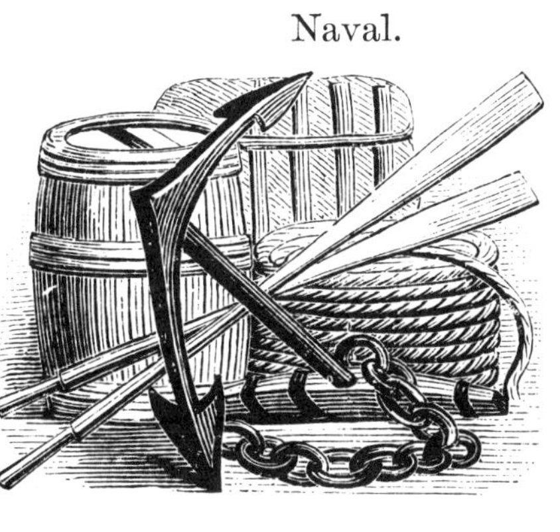

Odd-Fellows.

Optician.

Oyster-house.

Painter. (House)

Painter. (Sign)

Dry Goods.

Express.

Farmer.

Fish-dealer.

Fishing-tackle.

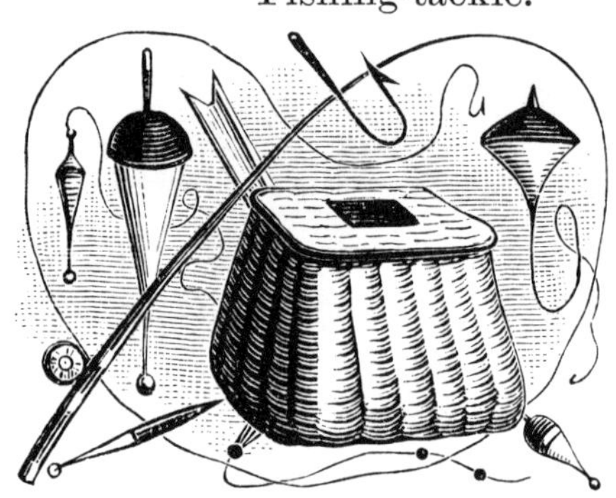

Florist.

Flour and Feed.

Fruit.

Furniture.

Furrier.

Gent's Furnishing.

Glover.

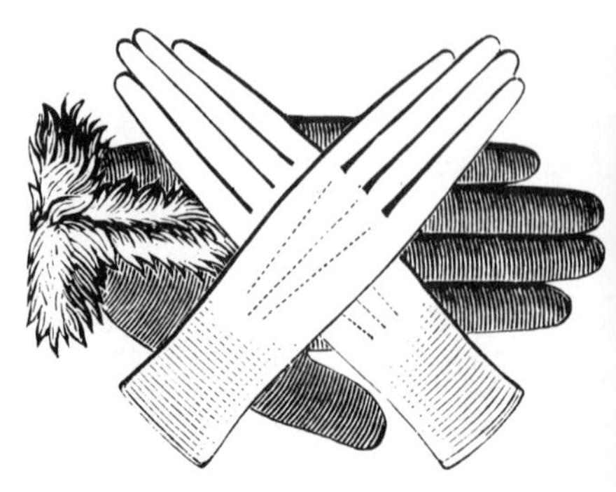

Grocer.

Gunsmith.

Hair-dresser. (Gent's)

Hair-dresser. (Ladies')

Hardware.

Harness-dealer.

Hatter.

Horse-dealer.

Horseshoer.

Hosiery.

Ice.

Jeweler.

Paper-hanger.

Patriotic.

Pawnbroker.

Perfumery.

Photographer.

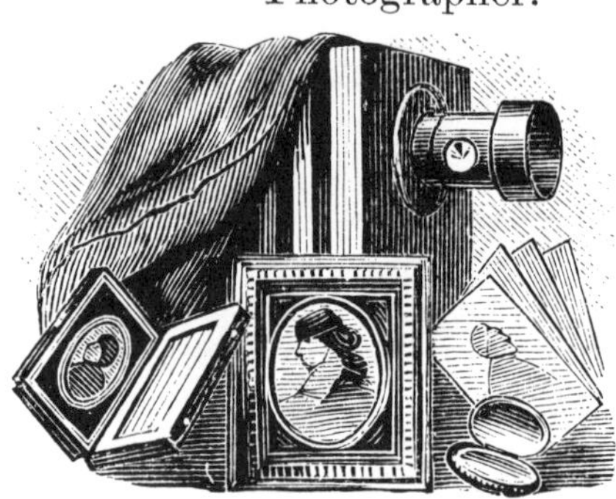

Piano-dealer.

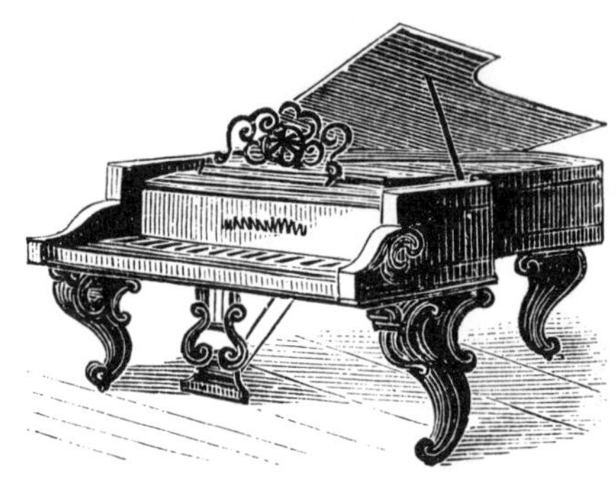

Pickles & Preserves.

Picture-Frames.

Plumber.

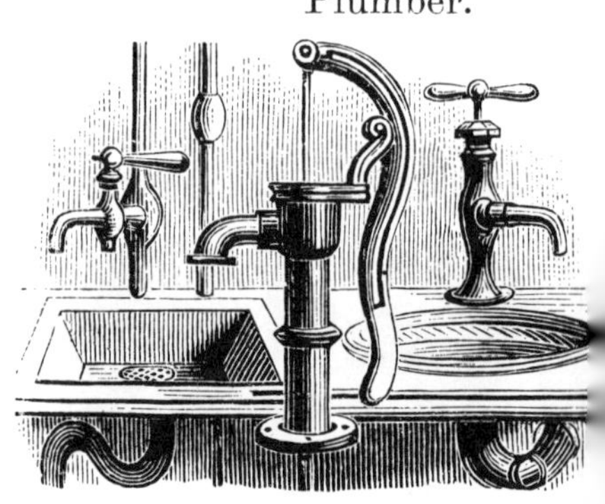

Printer. (Compositor)

Printer. (Press)

Race. (Boat)

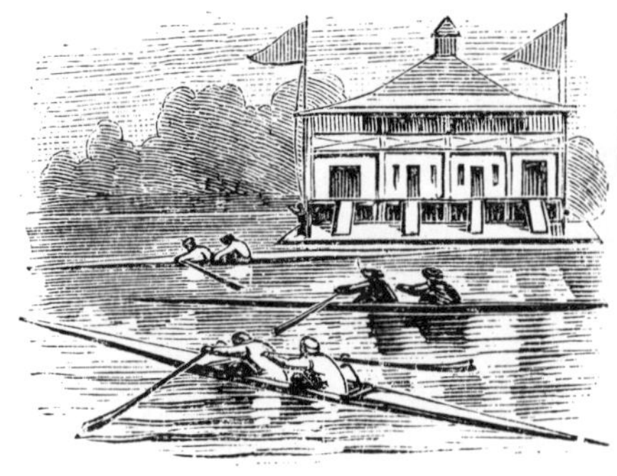

Race. (Horse)

Race. (Yacht)

Sashes, Blinds & Doors.

Scale-maker.

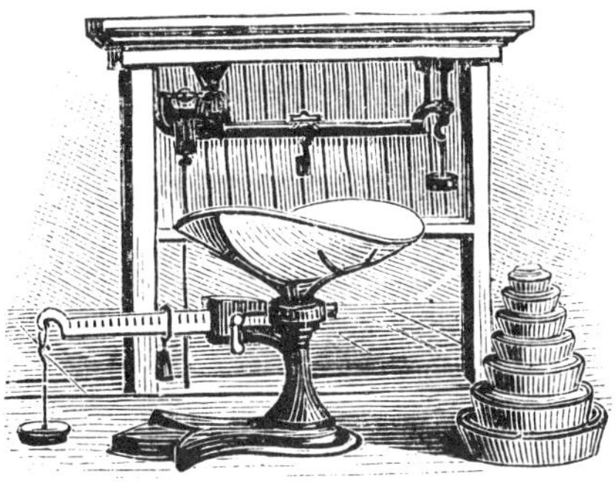

Schooner.

Railroad. (Freight)

Restaurant.

Segar-dealer.

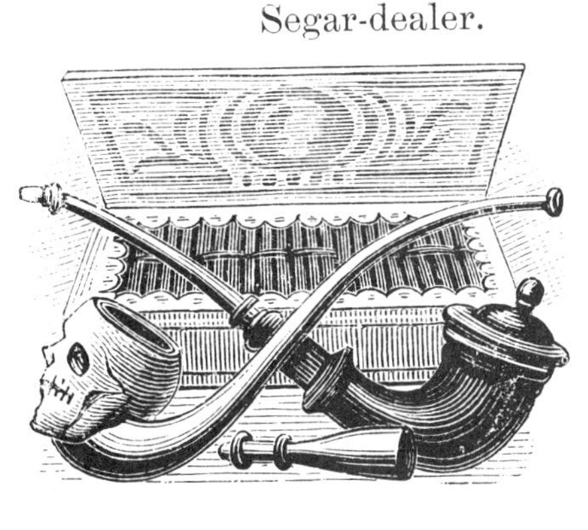

Sewing-Machines.

Shell-fish Dealer.

Ship-builder.

Ship-chandler.

Ship. (Clipper)

Shipping. (Freight)

Shoe-makers' Findings.

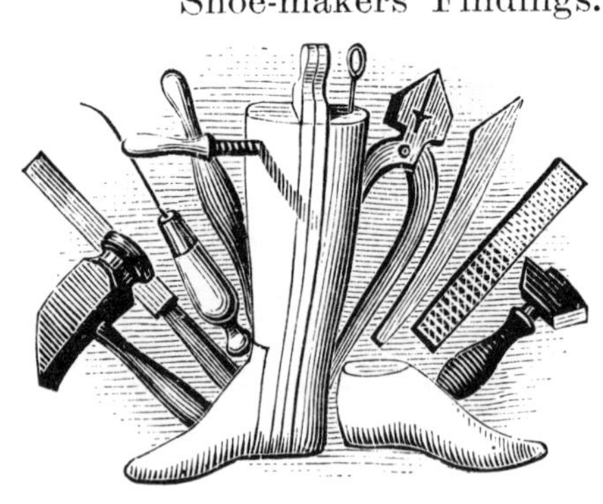

Silver-ware.

Sloop.

Soap and Candles.

Soda-water.

Stationer.

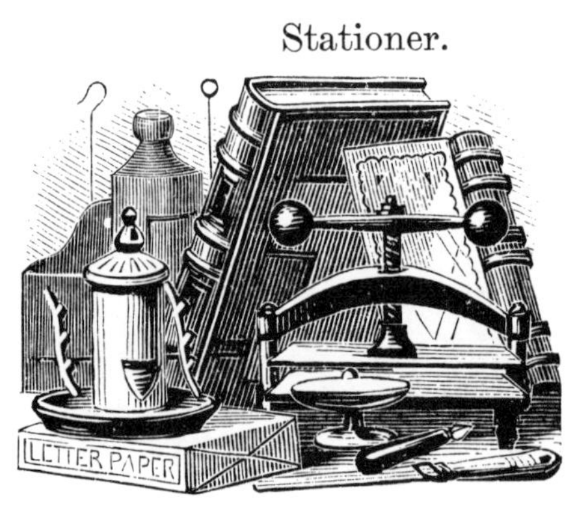

Steam-boat.

Steam-engine.

Steam-ship.

Steam-ship.

Stoves.

Surgical Instruments.

Tailor.

Tea-dealer.

Theatrical.

Tin-ware.

Tobacconist.

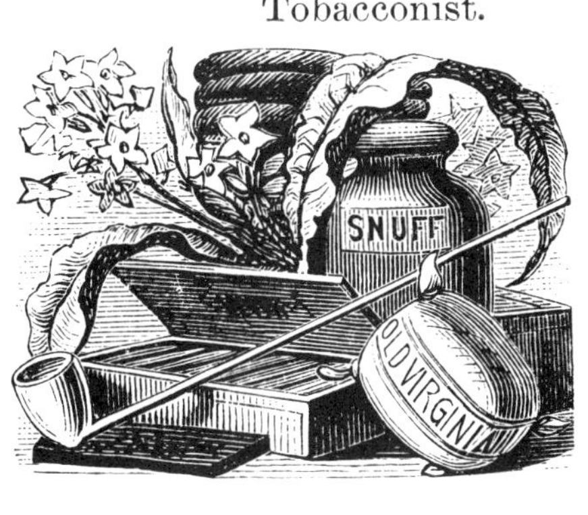

Toy-dealer.

Trunks.

Umbrella-dealer.

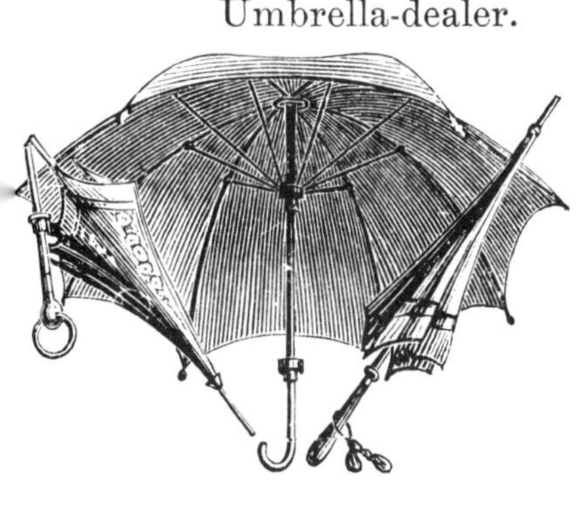

Undertaker.

Upholsterer.

Watches & Clocks.

Wheelwright.

Wine & Beer Garden.

Wine-dealer.

Willow-ware.

Wire-worker.

Wooden-ware.

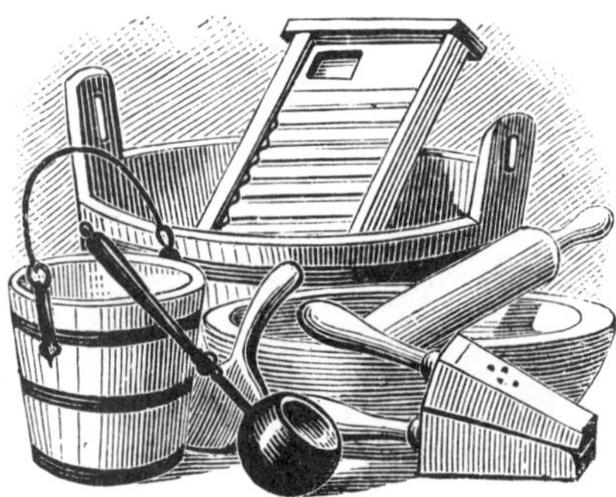

Yankee Notions.

Ornaments.